This book is a remembrance of law enforcement in Collier County,
Florida in the 60's, 70's, and thereabouts. It's a collection of cop
war stories, history, and outrageous events and is true and accurate
to the best of the author's recollection and/or what research allows.
Although the incidents depicted in these tales are true, some of the
people's names have been changed to protect the easily
embarrassed. Or, the true names have been lost to history. In some
cases composite characters were used. Except for cops. Most of
their names are genuine, except where noted as otherwise.

Other Books By G.D.Young

"I'm Peddlin' As Fast As I Can"

"Peavey's Paradise"

Available at your book seller
or on-line

Cover Illustration by the Author, G.D.Young

THANK YOU

No one writes a book on their own. The contributions by
others are many. I wish to thank the following folks
for their essential help in this project.

*First, my wife Sandy, who acts as my proofreader, editor, spell
checker and memory--in many cases.*

*Chester and Marta Keene who contributed every
photo in this work not attributed to others. Chester
is also a grand storyteller of tales
of yesteryear.*

*Dave Dampier who lived many of these events
with me,*

and

*Mike Grimm, Chief Ben Caruthers, Ray Barnett, Dave Johnson,
Harold Young, Gail Addison, Mike Gideon, Lila Zuck, Tom Smith,
and Bill Gonsalves.*

Plus any others I may have overlooked.

TO Jim & FRANCES
ENJOY.

NAPLES 5-OH
COPS, CROOKS, and CODGERS

By

Dedication

To my brothers and sisters:
The Cops

ABOUT THE COVER

We had a local wag named Jack. Jack was one of the first people I met in Naples and was a constant source of entertainment for those

who had the pleasure of his company.

Jack once broke a limb--or had some malady that required a wheel chair. A consumer of liquid stupid who liked to be out and about, he is the only person I can recall that was arrested for Driving Under the Influence in a wheelchair.

Jack had an old hound named Boneparte who roamed the Naples downtown area daily, begging treats and generally just keeping current on events. When a "leash law" was passed, Jack complied with the ordinance by hooking a leash to

Boneparte's collar, allowing the hound to continue on his rounds alone, the leash dragging behind him. And no one ever complained.

Choir Practice
Session One

Choir Practice? What the. . . ? *Choir Practice* is Cop slang for a get-together after a watch or shift ends. It can be anywhere, but places where the Cops are free of public scrutiny are preferred. There was a certain spot over by the Naples Bay that NPD officers liked.

At Choir Practice, the events of the watch were usually rehashed--War Stories--and everyone was relaxed and told it like it really was. That's what we'll be doing here. It's all true although a few names may have been changed to protect the guilty or easily embarrassed. So, please enjoy. It's a rare opportunity to eavesdrop on the way things really were way back then. And, probably still today.

THE KAW-LIGA KAPER When Hank Williams wrote about the troubles of poor ol' Kaw-liga, he overlooked one. So we'll make the record complete.

Our Kaw-liga was a life-size wooden Indian that stood outside a tobacco shop on Park Street. Each morning the shop's owner would take the wooden warrior out of his shed, attached to the outside of the shop, and wheel him around to the front of the store. On closing, it was back in the shed. He led a pretty uneventful life until he ran into Gunzan Rozes, a rookie NPD cop.

Gunzan, assigned to the midnight watch, was struggling through his initiation onto the force. All rookies were teased and aggravated and some took it better than others. When the veterans found out Gunzan was "goosey" his initiation took a whole new turn.

One early AM. when the town was locked down and cops were struggling to keep awake, Gunzan became the focus of fun and games.Working downtown, he was on foot, "rattling doors." This is cop jargon for checking the back doors of businesses to insure they are locked. As he crept down a darkened alley, one covert cop threw an empty garbage can behind him, the crash and roll evoking in Gunzan pure terror and gastric distress. When he finally was able to catch his breath, he was amped up, his hand on his revolver. He squinted and roved the alley with his flashlight beam, trying to penetrate the spooky nooks and crannies.

When he got near Park Street, another cop kicked the shed door of the tobacco shop, then jumped out of sight. Gunzan crept up to the door and, gun drawn, yanked it open. There he faced poor 'ol Kaw-liga standing in the darkness, arm up, tomahawk in hand. Gunzan fired one shot into Kaw-liga's belly before he realized he was killing a statue. He quickly shut the door and beat it out of the area. All the prankster cops did, too.

There was no report of the incident and none was asked for by Gunzan's superiors. The story became a legend, circulating around the PD for years. But no one would ever own up to being the garbage can slinger/door kicker or Gunzan Rozes. And I'm damn sure not gonna break the tradition now.

HEAVY'S FERTILE FEET   Cops get to see folks at their best and worst. And some characters that just make you scratch your melon and wonder under which category of human being they should be listed.

There was such a dude who was called Heavy, because of his size I imagine. He was just reasonably tall, but thick, his wrists and ankles like 4x4's. He was also a drunkard and brawler and thief, earning him frequent vacations in our jail.

For his health's sake, it was probably a good thing as he was filthy beyond belief, the stench intolerable. When he came to the hoosegow, we'd hose him down and clean him up as best we could so the other inmates wouldn't gag and heave up their weenies and beans.

Once, during this process, he removed his rotten work boon-dockers, and the sickening stink caused strong men to stagger and fall back. When told to remove his socks, he tugged at them but the foot part remained in place. On closer inspection we found he'd worn the socks so long, without removing them, they'd grown to his feet. Yep, grown to his feet. We had to take him to the hospital to have them removed. (The doctor soaked them and scraped them off a little at a time.)

Another time, during booking, he was removing the contents of his crusty wallet, and among the cards was a huge Palmetto bug. He gently took it out and put it on the counter as though it was a pet. Noting our stares he said, "What? I lives with 'em."

Thereby removing all doubt that what we suspected was certainly true.

NPD'S PRISON RELEASE PROGRAM At the old Naples Police Building, at 8th and 8th South, the parking lot was in rear, by the gas pumps. There was no rear door from the PD to the lot, requiring you to exit the front and hoof around the building. Inconvenient, and cops don't like that. So it was decided a door needed to be cut in the back wall, next to the parking lot.

As always, there was no money for the project. But, there was free labor available from the inmates. More specifically, the trustees, who could be let out of their cell with a reasonable expectation they wouldn't catch the next Bloodhound Bus to Slick City. At the time we had only one who met the criteria.

Hershel Hump, we'll call him, was a good ol' boy who was a victim of love. The love of booze, hooch, liquid stupid. He wasn't a pure dunce, but he wasn't going to be designing any rockets either. When he got a full gut of the Anchor Lounge's finest swill, he'd do anything. His last misadventure was DUI. He'd left the Anchor and made it four blocks to Four Corners, where he dutifully stopped for a red light. And waited. And passed out behind the wheel, earning him three months in the Bastille, of which he had 6 weeks remaining.

Chief Ben Caruthers told Hershel that if he'd cut a doorway thru the back wall, he could go home as soon as he was finished. Hershel jumped at the proposition and, with a two-pound hammer and concrete chisel, commenced with vigor.

Trouble was, the City Jail had been built to Federal Prison standards. The exterior walls were one-foot thick crammed full of reinforcing bars. At the end of the first day he'd excavated a hole about as big as a hamster's nest.

Hershel could've made a better deal if he'd waited a few years until the Sheriff's new jail was constructed. Some of the laborers on that project, figuring one day they'd probably be residents, mixed the mortar about ninety-percent sand and ten-percent cement. And they hid hacksaw blades in the mortar joints. The first night the jail was open, several convicts scraped out the mortar joints with spoons and escaped.

Not so the Naples Jail whose walls were poured concrete. So hard that Hershel was still pecking well into his fifth-week. And he'd only chipped out a hole big enough to allow the passage of a fat dog. With the prospects of him having to make life before the project was completed, some industrial saws were rented. And some welding torches to cut the steel. And Hershel finally made it back to the Anchor.

As irony would have it, when the new back door was completed, Hershel was one of the first customers to pass thru it. On his way back to jail.

THE MAYOR OF McDONALD'S QUARTERS Naples shameful ghetto, McDonald's Quarters, didn't have a city council member but they did have a "mayor." His name was Splitcoat. Though I, nor any of the old time cops I've asked remember his real name, everyone remembers Splitcoat.

He looked like the wonderful actor Tim Moore who played Kingfish on the TV version of Amos n' Andy. Once he told Dave Dampier how he got that name. As a young man, in the 40's, he was the proud owner of a zoot suit. One of those atrocities with baggy, pegged trousers and a swallow-tail coat. He wore it to a carnival one night.

Playing the game where you throw a baseball and try to knock over a pyramid of wooden milk bottles, he would vigorously wind up, causing the tails on his coat to flap in the breeze. The attendant crowd began to yell, "Go Splitcoat, Go." The name stuck.

Splitcoat, who lived across the street from Rabbit's juke, and two doors down from the Dew Drop Inn, supplemented his Social Security check by running a card game. Although illegal, we turned our heads unless it got rowdy and dangerous. One night I received a call from hiz zonner, asking for my presence at his house.

"They won't lets me cut the pot," he complained, tears in his eyes. Cutting the pot is when the proprietor of the game takes an amount from each pot to pay the overhead. Just like they do in Vegas.

"I'm not the one to tell about it," I explained, "it's against the law for you to even be running that game."

"But, I only wants a dime a hand." he persisted. "I pays the rent, buys the beer, and cuttin' the pot a dime a hand is fair."

I had to agree. So I left the law on the front porch, and went inside and told the players to give Splitcoat his damn dime.

Splitcoat loved fish head soup and when I could turn up a few snook heads at the pier I'd take them to him. A Porterhouse steak wouldn't have been met with a happier reception. He'd start to work, getting all the meat off the bones--eyes and all-- put it in a pot with his fixin's and pretty soon it was boiling. Never worked up the nerve to try any, but it did smell good.

His language was sprinkled with Splitcoatisms. "The hurrier I goes, the behinder I gets," he'd say. Or my favorite, "Everybody wants to go to Heaven, but nobody want to die."

I can still see him on the front porch of his hovel, rocking in his chair and surveying his domain, the squalid curtilage of McDonald's Quarters.

HOMEMADE HIGH TECH Chief Ben Caruthers was always inventive at getting what we needed. Since we never had any money for extras, it was usually by horse trading. Or diverse means.

He cut a deal with the FBI's Miami office to use our pistol range. In return, they furnished us with practice ammo. And they were very liberal with their free training for the NPD.

There was other stuff Ben arranged for us. Our Detective was the photographer, too. And the Crime Scene dude. It was one of the things you had to learn to do when you were assigned that job. Take the photos, develop them, and print them. Trouble was our equipment was old and terrible and there was no place to get proper training.

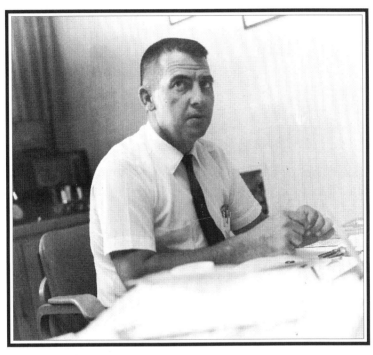

Ben made some deal with Kodak--don't know what--and soon I received personal lessons from a Kodak teacher, an enlarger appeared out of nowhere, and I had enough free film to open a photo store.

When Ben heard about shotgun mikes, he had to be more inventive. A shotgun mike would allow a person to listen to conversations from a long distance. Great for surveillance! It was a bundle of different length tubes, that you aimed at the target. The tubes resonated at different frequencies and sucked the sound in, where a small amp sent it thru earphones to the listener. We had to have one but they cost thousands. So Ben went to work.

We scrounged up a schematic out of a magazine. Ben found an aluminum supplier in town who almost gave us the tubing. We used a cheap Radio Shack solid state amp and mike. Having experience in electronics, I went to work putting it together. When it was finished, we went over to Cambier Park to test it.

Worked great! If you wanted to hear birds. We could hear a Purple-Butted Burbler a 100 yards away. People conversing? Nothing. I went back and checked the plans. That's when I found the magazine was a bird watching rag. It was supposed to heighten bird sounds. Finally, by adjusting tube lengths, we got it to work on human voices.

But, there were times when the clandestine conversations of surveillance subjects were interrupted by the tepid tweeting of a Tufted Titmouse. Or whatever avian happened to be a little off-key that day.

YOU CAN'T DO WHAT? When we used to gather at 4 Corners, in the early morning, we'd play a little game. We'd watch the North bound and South bound cars and see if anything about them made us suspicious. The way the driver looked or wouldn't look at us. Was he driving too slow. How was the car riding? Too low on the springs, indicating he might have a load of stolen goods in the trunk.

Some of us, like Byron Tomlinson, were experts at this game. Byron said the hair would stand up on his neck when there was something that wasn't righteous about the vehicle or driver. And a great majority of the time he was right.

We were trying to develop "cop's intuition", an extra sense that allows you to quickly survey a situation and just know that something is wrong. All good cops develop this skill. It saves their lives. And others.

I'm glad my days on the job are over. I wouldn't be allowed to use that skill today. It's called profiling, and in our suicidal politically correct world it's supposed to be a bad thing.

I just hope the cops, and the folks at the airports, use it anyway and lie about how they knew they had an A-hole on their hands.

We always did.

Trouble is, to be politically correct, they have to waste time checking grandma when they know they should be concentrating on young, middle-East males. Got to be politically correct. It's time we drop all that crap. Concentrate on the suspect group and if they don't like it, let 'em travel by camel next time.

MASON-DIXON MIXIN' It took almost a year to be hired by Chief Ben Caruthers at the NPD. Just weren't any openings. And Ben was picky. He'd been stung before trying to fill openings in a hurry and didn't want it to happen again. When the time finally came for a final--I hoped--interview I sat across his desk and he shuffled and reviewed my file. He confirmed several items then asked me, "You're from Charleston, West Virginia, right?"

"Yes, Sir," I said.

"Is Charleston above or below the Mason-Dixon Line?"

"It runs right through West Virginia," I said, "and Charleston is below it. And if you're wondering, my family fought for the Confederacy--Kanawha Rifles commanded by General George Patton's paternal grandfather. His name was George Patton, too."

Ben smiled. "I know it may seem silly, but in the South things like that can make a difference. When can you come to work?"

I didn't understand at the time but later on it became clear. Naples then still had segregation. Segregation with some unusual twists. A black could not come over from the Quarters on the East side of US 41 to the West side after 11PM. Unless, they had a job that required attendance at that hour. The bathrooms and water fountains in many establishments were marked "White Only", just like in Birmingham or Biloxi. Although the town was the bastion of Yankees it was still the Old South in many regards.

Although I never saw Ben display bigotry in any form, he was wise enough to know that it might be difficult for a Yankee lad to enforce some of ordinances and traditions that a Southerner would be used to.

What I didn't tell Ben was that there was no segregation in Charleston, W.Va. What little had been in place ended in 1956.

HIRSUTE ADORNMENT Back when Joe Citizen could grow all the hair he wanted and beard-up until he resembled *ZZTop* cops were stuck with a grooming guide that was akin to that used by the military. No sideburns further down than the center of the ear, neatly trimmed hair not hanging over the collar, no facial hair, you get the idea. Trouble was I was a Detective trying to blend into the crowd and my neat and clean look caused me to stand out like the Pope in a biker bar. I'd already won the war about sport coats and low bid, make that obvious unmarked police cars. They let me wear sport shirts with the tail out covering badge and gun, and let me buy a sweet little Chevy II hot rod that would outrun anything in town. But the hair thing was getting in my way.

So one day I showed up at work with a weekends worth of stubbly on my upper lip. All the cops chastened me that I was gonna get a kick in the ass. *No mustachios were allowed!* But not one supervisor said a thing. And so it grew. And grew, a polite Clark Gable type to begin with but still the forbidden hirsute adornment.

When the other cops saw that I had defied tradition and lived, other mustaches began to sprout. Finally, the administration realized that the rule was probably silly to begin with so it was changed to read: *Neatly trimmed mustaches are allowed so long as the ends do not extend lower than the corner of the mouth.* I immediately started growing a Fu Man Chu extension. And the floodgates were open!

Pictured above is yours truly with the original--I am told--NPD mustache. How would you like to have this Ahole on your case? Later, Dave Dampier went completely berserk with a Frito Bandito handlebar model. Then, even later, he is shown riding a motorcycle and sporting a full beard. He did have an excuse as it was Swamp Buggy Days and a beard was traditional.

Va-room, Va-room

Choir Practice
Session Two

THE PAW PAW PATCH

Naples first Jail, with two cells, was built in the 1940's at a cost of $386.68. It was located off of 8th Street South, in the general area of the Old Cove and the old Naples Hotel. Named the Paw Paw Patch, the inmates shared the facility with the voracious skeeters that were ubiquitous at the time.

Passers-by could often hear the plaintive calls from the Jail, *"Please Mr. Cale, let me out, the skeeters are killin' me."* Cale Jones was Chief at the time.

Another popular shout out was to children who passed by. Inmates would give them a quarter and ask them to go to the Beach Store and buy them a pack of cigarettes.

As you can see from the photo, the screen is ripped open. Years later, the window, in that exact condition, was delivered to me at the NPD. "Doc" Johnson, who apparently tore down the old jail, donated it as a piece of memorabilia from a Naples far in the rearview mirror. We stored it for several years until I was leaving the agency. I called the Museum and asked if they'd like to have it. They said yes, eagerly. A few years later, I asked what they'd done with it. They replied: "We misplaced it."

PIN-UP DOORS   Having two excuses not to do much--being retired and morbidly lazy--I don't do manual labor unless I can find an industrious illegal alien. But, I installed door pins on my sliding

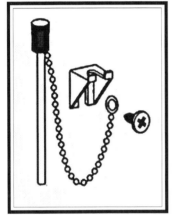

glass doors. With good reason. Being a cop you see things routinely that normal folks would think are impossible. One that caused me to do the extra work of installing door pins--really an easy job-- happened in the Coquina Sands area.

An enraged man was locked out of the house by a young woman. The house had two sliding glass doors installed which the woman had locked. No problem! The crazed man, adrenaline pumping, just lifted the sliding glass doors out of their frame, came in the house, and killed the woman.

He did what? Just as I said, he lifted the doors up, over the bottom sliding track, then out of the frame. *Just like they are installed.* And if you don't pin them together, any burglar or intruder can do that to yours. But spending a few minutes with a drill and a screwdriver, installing the simple device pictured above, can prevent that.

The pins are available at any hardware store or locksmith and aren't expensive--just a few bucks. Installing them is no trouble if you follow the instructions and don't drill into the glass.

The best method is to pin the two or three doors together, then pin one to the door frame. That way, when they try to pry them up the doors aren't going anywhere vertically because they're locked to the door frame. They're not, of course, going anywhere horizontally, either.

We have two sliding glass doors, and just use one. The other is never open. So, the pin in it--to the frame--is never removed. Except, maybe, in some sort of emergency.

So pick up a couple pins, get out your tools, and start screwing.

AUTHOR'S NOTE: I remember this homicide so well because we had a family vacation planned and I knew we couldn't--in good conscience--leave town until it was solved. I didn't say anything about it because it was a given: the Chief doesn't leave town when there's a lunatic on the prowl. I'd probably have to cancel the trip. One of my Detectives, unasked, worked day and night until he caught the murdering scumbag. He gave me a call in the middle of the night saying, "Go ahead on vacation, Chief, we got him." The Detective's name was Irv Stoddard.

BASHERS About the time The Moorings was near build-out and Park Shore was getting underway, it became a fad, among high school morons, to engage in mailbox bashing. The damage was inflicted by cruising by a mailbox, having a passenger lean out the window and destroy a mailbox with one swing of a baseball bat.

Since it was a hit-and-run crime, the imbeciles were hard to catch. Occasionally, one would catch themselves. One memorable dope tried to use his fist instead of a ball bat and ended up in the ER with a mangled paw. Another genius leaned out too far, looking for the box, and found it with his thick skull. You can see the level of intelligence we were dealing with here but, still, they were difficult to catch in the act.

Finally the victims began to retaliate. Up in Pine Ridge the fools added to the destruction by running over the box *and* post. The flimsy aluminum posts bent over easily, and the box was squashed under the car. To counteract this, some of us put our mailboxes on sawed-off telephone poles, set in concrete. Shortly thereafter, a dufuss, who tried to run over one of these, was launched through the windshield after the sudden stop--a Jeep vs a telephone pole being no contest.

Another popular sport was "burning" a lawn. This was done by driving a car onto the grass at high speed, then slamming on the brakes, the resultant skid ripping up the lawn. Corner lots were particularly susceptible. Residents tried to stop this by placing large boulders in the swale. Unfortunately, the swale was owned by the City who couldn't allow these hazards or the attendant liability.

One day we received a call from an outraged repeat victim. He wanted us to inspect his *protective measures*. In his front yard we found steel spikes driven in the ground at two-foot intervals. They protruded from the ground about 4 inches. "Let 'em burn me now," he growled. We explained that his *probable* victim, would be a yardman, or neighborhood child who was accidentally impaled in his spike garden. And said victim would soon relieve him of the worry of protecting his home, because they'd *own* it, awarded by the civil courts. Our homeowner, a retired Army Major, saw our point and removed the spikes. He wasn't, however, finished.

Soon we rushed to his home on Crayton Road where a vehicle was stopped in the middle of the street, with two teenagers huddled nearby, terrified and trembling. The vehicle bore the ragged holes made by shotgun pellets, shot at an angle. The Major stood nearby, gloating.

"Bet they'll think twice about bashing mailboxes and burning lawns now," he said. And he was correct. Most of the vandalism ended that night.

Doesn't take long for word to get around that if you go out smashing and bashing there might be a wild old coot waiting in the bushes. With a 12 gauge shotgun loaded with double-O buck. That he'd use to blow your doors off.

THE AMAZING, INFLATABLE, $300 DRESS   It was 1965 and we'd received a shoplifting complaint from a dress shoppe in the 3rd Street South shopping area. It was, of course, *The Season* because, at the time, the exclusive area was only open then. Closed all summer. Most all the other shops in town could've, too, since they made the majority of their profits from the Snowbirds. The other stores did close, during the summer, on Wednesday afternoons.

Howsumever, I went to the shoppe (*shoppe* meaning expensive) that we'll call Snob's, owned by a lady I called Zazu. Zazu was torqued because a fat woman had walked out with one of her cocktail dresses and had given Zazu a menacing look when she tried to follow her. The thief'd left in a black Cadillac. This wasn't much help since most of the shoppers on 3rd Street South were from Port Royal and in Port Royal there were a lotta fat ladies in Cadillacs.

While filling out my report, I asked Zazu how much the dress cost. *"Three-hundred-dollars,"* she said. I said, "Was that what you paid for it? That's what your loss really is."

Zazu mumbled and grumbled for a while and told me she'd have to look it up and get back with me. She didn't. Not even after a couple weeks, so I dropped by Snob's to give her some inspiration.

I explained to her that I had to have the number or her insurance wouldn't pay. She said it wasn't worth turning into insurance, anyway. She hadn't paid that much for it.

I told her there must be a helluva profit in dresses but I still needed a number so I could determine if the theft was a misdemeanor or a felony--fifty-dollars was the dividing line. I finally squeezed it out of her.

"Truth is, these *Zazu Originals* aren't quite that. I go over to Miami to *Jackson-Byron's Bargain Basement* and buy them there. Then I bring them back and sew a Zazu Originals label in them."

"So how much money did you have in it?" I asked.

With downcast eyes she whispered, "About fifteen-dollars." Then, trying to legitimize this dubious commerce, she said, "They don't care anyway. They're only going to wear it to a cocktail party one time, tell everyone they paid $300 dollars for it, then donate it to one of those charity re-sell stores, over on 10th Street, and claim a *$400 tax deduction.*"

That pretty much solved the case for me. I wouldn't be busting my arse on this one. Couldn't determine, in this whole moral dung pile, who was the *bigger* damn thief.

THE 5th AVENUE SOUTH SHUFFLE   We had a con man who used to visit Naples every year--like the Asian flu and the creeping crud. He had a sweet little scam that was simple, effective, and would pull him in a couple hundred a day. In the mid-sixties that was good bucks, considering I wasn't making much more than that *a month*. His scam worked like this.

He loved the many gift shops on 5th Ave South. In the shop, he'd select a greeting card and take it to the counter. There, he'd explain that it was his daughter's birthday and he, a traveling salesman, was

19

going to miss it. But, he could send a pretty card and he wondered if the clerk had a nice, clean, crisp twenty he could put inside. The clerk always obliged.

Our villain would take the twenty, seal it in the card, and put the card in his inside sport coat pocket. Then, he'd reach for his wallet.

"Durn," he'd mutter, "left it in the car. But, no problem, I'll just run out and get it." Saying that, he'd take the card from his inside pocket, put it on the counter and say, "Hold that 'til I get back."

And the clerk would, many times until the end of the workday. Then they'd rationalize the customer had gone somewhere else, or whatever, and open the card to retrieve the money. There they found a folded piece of blank card stock. And no money.

Our Slicky-boy had, of course, had two cards in his coat pocket. The new one with the money and his prop to leave on the counter.

Some days he'd hit three or four stores on 5th Ave before he left for, well, *greener* pastures. He always made Bonita his next stop and always came from Miami, via Marco Island. Lacking computers back then, we couldn't trace him any further.

It took a few years to nail him and when we did it was with *modern* technology.

That we invented.

MORE SHUFFLIN' It was the "Season" again and the con men, forgers, and now, counterfeiters, were giving us more gray hair than Jay Leno. We'd try to give the businesses a *heads up* when we became aware of a particular weasel, but, in those days before computer networks, we just weren't very effective.

Counterfeiters were a sporadic problem. When some crooked Rembrandt turned out some Primo plates or some creditable off-set printed fakes, there would be a flow for a while. When the clerks would finally figure out that the $20 dollar bills that didn't quite feel right, and had ink that smeared when you rubbed it, and all had the *same serial number*, were bogus, then counterfeiters would move on.

At the time there weren't any magnetic threads, or iridescent inks, or watermarks to help clerks insure that a bill was genuine. And, it being the Season, the clerks were harried and most didn't even try to pick out bad bills. Some were worse than others.

I took a bogus bill, that had been turned in with the regular receipts by a market on 5th Avenue South, back to the store. Showing it to the manager, he said he just couldn't understand how that could happen. His clerks diligently inspected all twenties (the most popular bill to counterfeit). I asked if I could try an experiment. He okayed it.

I went to the checkout counter and asked for a pack of cigarettes. The clerk handed me a pack and and I handed her a counterfeit twenty. Not *just* a bogus twenty, but one that had been stamped with red ink, in half-inch letters, twice on each side *COUNTERFEIT*. She immediately took it and gave me my change. I think the manager might still be sputtering.

So, we were being hammered by the bad guys--and gals--and still weren't making much of a dent in the crime rate. But, we finally figured out how to kick some criminal butt.

THE PYRAMID SCHEME Some wise soul at the Naples PD--don't remember who--decided that to catch con men you needed to use their methods. One of the most famous was the Pyramid game. Also called *8 Ball, Dinner Party, Airplane* and many others, it claimed that a donated sum would be returned ten or twenty times over. In fact, about 90% of the participants would lose money. All but the *Slicksters* who started the game.

What was intriguing was the mathematics. One person contacted two, these two, two more making four, and so on, rapidly increasing the number of persons involved. The wise one who converted the con game to our use--probably a Dispatcher--saw how this could vastly improve our telephonic warning system.

It worked like this: When we received info that a counterfeiter or card shuffler or forger was at work, our Dispatcher would call a specific merchant with the warning. This merchant would, in turn, warn two more, and so forth, just like the Pyramid Scheme. Soon every merchant in the area knew what was going down. And, after being stung so many times, they were damn sure ready for some payback.

We worked with the merchant's association to put the plan together. Each merchant was given a list with the two businesses they were to notify when they received a warning call. And did it work!

It wasn't long until when the Card Shuffler reached into his sport coat pocket to bring out the fake card, there was a detective waiting to receive it.

Again, the old saying proved true: *Necessity is a Mother.*

A REAL HERO   James Pugh had been a hero in the bloodiest battles of WWII. That torrid summer's night in the 1960's he showed that he hadn't forgotten how to do it.

I'd received a call that a certain, elusive, gent, who we had a warrant for, was partaking of liquid stupid in *Rabbit's Juke* in McDonald's Quarters. We'd been trying to serve the warrant for months, but our prey was slicker than Willie, himself. I tried to gather up some help, but everyone was out on calls, so I headed over there alone, telling dispatch to send help as soon as possible. This was really stupid, but I was young and afflicted with that condition.

Arriving at the Juke, and being in plain clothes, I thought I might be able to slip inside and mill with the sardine-packed crowd unnoticed. After all, it was after midnight, the Juke didn't waste any money on lights, and most of the patrons were addled by booze.

I spotted my man and sidled over to him. Putting a hand on his arm, I said, "You're under arrest. Come quietly. Let's get outta here."

He was too smart for that, announcing, "A city cop wants to take me to jail on some trumped-up charges. You gonna stand for that?"

You have to appreciate the times and conditions to gauge the impact of this statement. The civil rights rumblings had just begun. Many times overt friction between black people and whites was coming to the surface. This heat could cause the pot to boil over, especially in a bar full of drunks. The crowd immediately decided there wasn't any white cop gonna take any black brother to the city slammer. To insure it wasn't going to happen, they began to close in on me.

Just then a deep voice said, "This police officer is just doing his duty. And nobody is gonna stop him. If someone wants to try, they come through me first." It was James Pugh, suddenly at my side.

And Sir Galahad couldn't have been more welcome.

James, although far from a young man, was still thick and powerful, not someone you wanted to trifle with. And he had the respect of the community. The crowd decided they were going to let justice take its course and, in an instant I was stuffing the arrestee in my car.

I thanked James, and he just nodded and walked off. I know he had to realize what danger was involved in standing up to a drunken mob of your brothers when you know they're wrong. But he performed his civic duty like the true hero that he was.

James has been gone a few years now but I've never forgotten him. There are few made like that.

Rest in peace, kind sir.

PUSH MY BUTTON At the CCSO we were having a problem. Many of the doors had new *security* locks installed. They were of the push-button variety where you punched in a four number code. Problem was folks were always forgetting what code they'd programed in. There was a way you could over-ride it and open them, but that little reprograming tool wasn't available to anyone but Roger Fussell, the guy who ran Maintenance. And Roger was a busy guy, with nineteen buildings to worry about.

We began to wonder about the integrity of the system one day when I was in the hall talking to Roger. He had two trustees with him. Trustees were used extensively at the SO, and other jails, to save the taxpayers money. As an example, it took about twenty-five to run the kitchen each day. Plus more to do the daily building clean-up and maintenance. Roger always had two or three with him.

One of the trustees, looking at the door said, "those locks are worthless, you know."

"They're a pain in the keester," Roger said, "but worthless. . ?"

"Yep," said the trustee. "Bet I can open that one up not even knowing the code."

"Okay," Roger said accepting the challenge, "let's see you do it."

The trustee squatted down to lock level, then moved his head around, looking at the lock from different angles. Then he began typing in numbers, fingers flying. Within a minute the door was open.

"What the . . ?" Roger and I both said.

"Easy," the trustee explained. "People put in their four number code and use it for a long time. Door like this, in an office, probably has the code tapped in a hundred times a day. That causes the buttons to look like they've been shined, polished from the oil in people's skin. Looking at the keys in the right light, you can tell which ones have been punched the most. Pick the four most used keys, then it's just a matter of typing in four number sequences until you hit the right one. No problem."

For me, even the possible combinations with four numbers was too much. But for a burglar, it didn't seem much of a deterrent.

Before that, I'd been thinking of putting one of those locks on my garage door. I changed my mind.

BAD BIRD Once Mike Grimm (see photo) and I were at Lineback's Firestone getting new tires on our unmarked cop car. Inside the waiting room, we noticed that Paul had acquired a new *helper*. A Mynah bird. Paul'd placed him in a cage up by the front door. He hoped the bird would be an attraction, something for his customers to smile at.

He certainly made Mike and me smile, being a perfect mimic and a quick study. And, he seemed to know just when to say something, not just jabber at random.

Dave Johnson later told me that when he was a child on Marco Island the family had a Mynah bird named Sinbad that was so smart it was disconcerting. He said the bird was placed close to the bathroom door, and whenever anyone occupied the facilities, the bird would mimic the sound of gastric explosions, then emit a satisfying, "Aaaaaaah."

He'd also, when placed on the back porch, aggravate the neighbors dog by yelling "*Here Spot, come and eat,*" in a perfect imitation of poor Spot's master's voice. The dog would race around the yard until he collapsed from exhaustion, trying to find out just where in hell his boss was.

Paul Lineback's bird was similarly disposed to rude humor as we found out, after spending some time with him, improving his vocabulary.

An unhappy Paul called us one day ranting, "You've ruined my bird. He's running off all my customers."

Inquiring how, Paul went on. "When a customer comes in, he yells at them, '*Buy something you cheap son-of-a-bitch.*' And there's no need of you guys denying it 'cause he sounds just like Mike Grimm."

PAYBACK IS A BITCH   If Ed had been a wrestler, he'd have been labeled *Haystack* or *Man Mountain* or, at least, *Big Ed*. Because that he was. About 300 pounds with a neck like a keg of nails and fingers like smoked sausages. Mostly muscle, too, from his years of pulling the nets in his trade as a fisherman.

Big Ed was a mean 'un, with a disposition like a gorilla with hemorrhoids. Not someone to trifle with. He was a regular customer of the NPD or Sheriff's Office, usually producing a legendary encounter.

Once Ed had possession of a skiff thats ownership was in dispute. The boat was resting in the water near Boat Haven. Cops were trying to figure how to get the boat started, so they could drive it to the ramp and up on their trailer when Big Ed arrived. He said he didn't have the keys with him, but that was no problem. And it wasn't. He just leaned over the seawall and lifted the boat, motor and all, up to dry ground.

Another time, we had a warrant to serve on him. It required that he go to jail and bond out. One of our biggest officers, Jack Bliss, went out to do the dirty work. Ed's tiny wife, Sweet Pea, greeted Jack at the door and warned him that Ed was asleep and didn't take kindly to being awakened. Jack told her he was just gonna have to be ticked off cause this *wouldn't wait*.

In the bedroom, he called Big Ed's name, eliciting no response. So, he put his hand on Ed's arm and shook him. Bad move. Ed spun around, clamped Jack's arm like a vice and said, "Don't mess with me when I'm sleepin'." Jack, in agony, replied, "No problem, Ed. I have a warrant for your arrest. When you get up, drop by the station and we'll process it." And that's how it worked.

Knowing all these tales, Dave Johnson, couldn't believe the message that was broadcast over his police radio. *Big Ed said he needs help, Sweet Pea is beating on him.* Sweet Pea, at about 110 pounds. Dave eagerly took the call. This was something he had to see.

He could hear Ed howling when he arrived on the scene. Going inside, he found Ed on the floor, his leg in a cast. Seems he'd broken it fishing. Standing over him was Sweet Pea, with an aluminum baseball bat, taking measured, hefty swings at the cast. She'd already busted it open and was now getting to Ed's beefy leg. He howled like a werewolf with each blow.

Dave, enjoying the sight, watched her deliver a little more agony, then stopped her. It seems Sweet Pea was playing catch-up for years of putting up with the brute. There's a lesson to be learned here.

That's the way it works with little women. Folks used to ask me who I was afraid of. "Sandy", I'd say. They'd laugh, Sandy, my wife, at just over 5 feet tall and 100 pounds, and me six feet and over 200. "It's true," I'd say. "Ever since she found out I had to sleep sometime, I've lived in fear."

Choir Practice
Third Session

THERE'S SOMETHING ROTTEN ABOUT HIS CASE

Old-timers remember when the airport, then entirely at Radio Road and Airport, was not just a terminal but a cluster of one story, barracks-type buildings. They'd been left there from WWII and afterwards used for most anything they could accommodate. Some folks even lived there. Gradually, they were torn down. During this process, one of my old associates and retired cop Chester Keene was sent there. It went like this, in his own words:

Someone had called in a *Signal-7* (dead body) at the airport. I arrived at the location and found an old aircraft being stripped down to be part of the off-shore artificial reef. Sitting about midway back was what appeared to be a corpse. It was sitting up, wearing a trench coat and ball cap. The cap rested atop a rotting head, the meat falling off and flies feasting. The detectives had already been there and the plane was fenced off with yellow crime scene tape to protect the evidence and keep people away. That was fine with me. The smell was horrendous.

We waited for the Medical Examiner, Dr Smith, to arrive so the next steps in the investigation could proceed. On scene, he hastened to the corpse, began picking at the head, then backed off and roared with laugher.

"You have something *dead* here, alright? he said, "a dead chicken."

"What?"

"A dead chicken. Someone has a strange sense of humor."

And he was right. On closer inspection, we found a rotting carcass sitting on top of the propped-up coat, and hidden by the ball cap. We wondered what was going on until we started filling out our report.

First line, Date: April 1st. We'd been had. *April Fool's Day.*

27

FLIP, FLOP, AND LIE The recent completion of work around I-75's Golden Gate interchange caused me to recall when it *should've* been completed. How about the early 80's, over twenty-years before. So what happened?

Original plans called for an interchange exactly where it *is* now, with connecting roads exactly where they *are* now. In conjunction with this project, it was recommended, by the State and federal traffic engineers, that parking on US 41, in downtown Naples, be eliminated. This, because engineers knew that I-75 would draw much more traffic to Naples and US 41 would need the extra lane created by removing parking. Pretty sound thinking and seemingly a done deal until some of our inglorious leaders got hold of it.

The NPD worked closely with the State in planning the project and one engineer, who we'll call Mac Grader, made many trips with extended stays working on same. Our first problem came with an explanation of the project to the City Council. It became obvious early that there was going to be opposition, led by a local "civic leader" we referred to as B.S. Overload.

B.S., and his misguided retinue, reckoned that we didn't want an interchange at Golden Gate because it would just funnel more folks into Naples. And Naples, at the time, was an advocate of the *Reverse* Field of Dreams dictum: If you *don't* build it they *won't* *come.* Let 'em get off in the County. Let them deal with 'em.

The County, being much more progressive at the time, heartily agreed. Glad to accommodate!

B.S. also argued that if the G Gate interchange wasn't built, there wouldn't be any need to ban parking on US 41. He was against that plan because it would create a "speedway." And the merchants needed the parking for customers.

Mr Overload was such a pain in the rumble seat, we scheduled a meeting, to try to better explain our proposition. He readily agreed.

Mac explained why the project was needed, and if not now, soon after--at much greater expense. B.S. would have none of it. As the meeting was breaking up, he took me aside and said, "You better get your partner to change his plans or I'll change them for him." That was it.

Mac, of course, would have none of that. Besides the money already invested it was just dumb thinking. Two days later he

28

changed his mind.

Mac came into my office and dropped into a chair like a load of wet rocks. "Where's Palatka?" he asked. "Somewhere in Poland?"

"Don't know," I said, "maybe up around Jacksonville someplace. Why?"

"Just got a call from my boss. I've been transferred there. Effective immediately."

And he was. And the interchange was eliminated and parking remained on US 41.

Sometime later I inquired of B.S. just what he'd done. He smiled, said, "Just takes one phone call, son. If you have the right number." And that was it.

But even the dumbest student is no longer left behind and, a few years later, B.S. realized he was wrong and reversed his position, leading the fight to remove parking from 41.

Then, he ran, successfully, for City Council, touting "*Elect the man who removed parking from US 41.*"

Evidently, having no shame is a political asset.

COUNCILMAN SPEAK WITH FORKED TONGUE

The recent sleazy, partisan, national politics surrounding the Health Care bill calls to mind some weasels we had on the local level. And there were/are several. Some of their acts so blatantly two-faced you wonder how they get away with it. But, they do, relying on the short memory of the voters.

One "lifer" County politician used to laugh at the voter's stupidity, saying their memory was only six- months long. He'd say he could take a crap on the Courthouse steps, in front of the Girl Scouts, and in six-months it would be forgotten. He may have had a point.

Another barfbag, showed total disregard for the public's ability to even *recognize* his disingenuous rhetoric. He was a City Councilman and we'll call him Ol' Split-tongue.

At the time, the union pot was boiling: to the workers making a hearty soup; to the City a witch's caldron. The City worker's doing the cooking were the police officers. Tired of the City's arbitrary and unfair policy regarding tenure, a strong pro-union push was underway.

The movement's momentum had grown until the City had to recognize it. A public forum was held in the City Council Chambers. Because of the overflow crowd, space was reserved for the "public." Police officers had to stand outside. Even those who lived in the City and were taxpayers and, therefore, the "public."

During one of the vigorous exchanges, Ol' Split-tongue reckoned that the City should identify all those cops pushing for a union and *fire* them, forthwith. This, of course, was the main reason a union was needed because such firings were, indeed, possible.

Howsumever, not ten-minutes later the meeting recessed. Ol' Split-tongue chose not to use the rear chamber exit and walked directly out the front door into the angry crowd. There had to be many there who, even though being locked outside, had heard what he'd said. But, standing on the top step, pumping his fist in the air, he shouted., "Give 'em hell boys, I'm with you." Then he gave a mock salute, and ambled away. Before the stunned crowd could compute what had just happened he was gone.

Ol' Split-tongue went on to win several more terms at this office-- and that--and was never called into account for being a frequent, notorious liar.

The shame in this country is we have come to *expect* politicians to act in this manner.

KING OF THE PACKRATS Dick Cooper, a cop I had the pleasure of working with at the NPD and CCSO, received a call from a concerned neighbor in Royal Harbor. Something was amiss with the man next door. Arriving on the scene, Dick saw the man in his yard, on his knees, behind a cheap push mower. His hands were still holding the mower's handle--a neat trick since he was stone dead.

Cooper made the appropriate calls, then went to see if there was anyone in the house. Opening the door, he could see into the kitchen. The kitchen table was shoved into a corner and on it was piled money--so much that some had slid onto the floor. Cooper entered.

The house was found to be vacant, and what Cooper discovered inside still, to this day, blows his mind. In the bedroom, the dresser had five dollar bills stacked on top. Opening the drawers, he found them packed full of fivers, rubber-banded in bundles, and marked as to amount. And that wasn't all!

The closets and dressers *throughout the house* were similarly packed. Shoe boxes in the closets stored tens, twenties, up to and including $100 bills. The final total was well over $800,000 dollars. *Cash money!* Ms Mamie Tooke was called at the Bank of Naples and arrangements made to store the load. Dick says it took a van to carry it off.

When Cooper checked the garage, he found the deceased also had a fondness for canned goods. Stacked up to seven-feet high, and sorted by contents, were tomatoes, peas, beans, you name it. All seemingly purchased when on sale and some stored so long the cans had rusted out and were seeping juice.

Not much was ever found out about this strange customer. No friends, family, known source of income.

The money was eventually converted to government use, none ever put to the arcane purpose for which it had been hoarded.

VOODOO? HOODOO? YOU DO? Everyone knows that Voodoo is just something scary in the movies. Right? That it can't hurt you. Keerect? That's true. *Unless you believe it.* Then it can kill you. A death spell placed on a true believer can cause that cursed soul to wither and die. Happens with regularity.

In our office, at the CCSO, Roger Fussell and I had displayed some artifacts taken from a Voodoo grave discovered in some remote area of Golden Gate. We had the small statue of Chango, who--if properly plied with sacrifices--will intercede with the divine gods that allow you into voodoo heaven. We also had a voodoo doll, a statuette of a black, female figure, some dried fruit and lizards, and the letter to Chango himself. All this had been sprinkled with chicken blood. (Our lab folks had checked)

There were people that came into our office who would take one look at the display, and do one of those *feet don't fail me now* moves. Some were police officers. One of the officers would, thereafter, cross the street if he saw me coming. He told other cops I was a devil. He was terrified of me.

In South Florida, people on the street that are practitioners of Santeria--Haitian Voodoo--are common. A ubiquitous mojo found in a bag tied around their necks is the forked bone from an possum's penis--a fertility enhancer.

And I know that some of us cops--and other bureaucrats--are *called* zombies. But a *cop* believing in Voodoo?

How do folks get in such a condition? What's the appeal? I just never could understand the fascination of Voodoo. Build a big fire, do the naked zombie dance with a bunch of lustful, writhing Voodoo priestesses. Guzzling aphrodisiacs until everyone ends up bumpin' uglies in a squirming orgy. Who would that appeal to?

THE HEAVYWEIGHT CHAMP OF NAPLES   In the late 1950's Scruff McGullis was the undisputed heavyweight champion. Of Naples. On Saturday nights. At *The Barn*, and other watering holes where fights were common, he reigned supreme.

Scruff wasn't particular. Every customer was subject to his abuse. And, if he wasn't too drunk, he was tough. Fisherman tough from a lifetime of pulling the nets.

On this evening, Scruff was disappointed. Try as he might he hadn't been able to provoke even a spirited shoving match. But, salvation was at hand.

He would've been much taller, the fella that walked up to the bar, maybe six-feet-three, if he wasn't so stoop-shouldered. His walk was splayfooted and his arms hung loose like broken lanyards. Right comical he was, too, with a shock of dark hair drooping over his forehead, a big nose, squinty eyes, and a mouth as wide as an Okeechobee bass. A perfect opponent!

Scuff leaned over the bar and asked the tender if he knew the stranger. "One of them actor fellas," the bartender replied. "Been in here a couple a times. Down here working on some TV show about cops in Tallahassee."

Scruff ordered another beer and stomped down to his proposed adversary.

The actor wasn't sitting on a stool, just resting his elbows on the bar, casual like. Scuff preferred to attack someone while they were sitting. But, he figured he could whip this clown on roller skates in a phone booth.

So, he made his overture: "Say, I hear tell you're one of them actors."

No response.

"I said," this time a little louder, "I heard you're one of them Hollywood actors."

The actor turned to Scruff, gave him a squint-eyed once over and said, "Actually, I'm from New York, and there are those in the business who would debate you on my acting prowess."

Big words. Big, fancy words with a Yankee accent. There was nothing that riled Scruff worse than fancy talk, unless it was a Yankee accent. He was really gonna enjoy this.

"I heard all you actors were queer," he said. "Queers or pre-verts, like to help sheep over the fence, and like that."

The actor sighed, put down his beer. "Okay," he said, "we've all enjoyed your witty repartee. Now, why don't you let me finish my drink in peace, and I'll be on my way."

Scruff laughed. "Bet you would, 'bout now, like to be on your way. But that ain't gonna happen 'less you go through me."

The actor smiled, "That being the case, perhaps we can engage in some genial conversation. Maybe you can answer a question for me. One that always arises when I meet a gentleman such as yourself."

Scruff frowned. "What kinda question?"

"I was just wondering, do little town's hire buffoons like you to be the village idiot, or do you volunteer as a public service?"

Scruff didn't know what a "buffoon" was, but he was damn sure familiar with "idiot." Rage rolled over him like a hurricane tide. He snorted, cocked his big right arm, started to fire it and . . . his lights went out.

Eyewitness accounts vary as to just what the actor hit Scruff with. Some say a left hook, others a straight right, still others the ol' one-two. All agreed on one matter: the punch had been fast and devastating. One second Scruff was in front of the actor, bowed up, ready to unleash lightening, the next second he was on his back, eyes wide open but seeing nothing. They also remember the actor's departure, gesturing as though tipping a hat, saying "Ladies, gentlemen, a fond adieu, and goodnight."

Scruff would later claim that it was a sucker punch—and a damn lucky one—that had put out his lights. In truth, he knew he'd been poleaxed with a killer blow delivered by someone who knew exactly how to do it.

Fact of the matter was, Scruff was right. It hadn't, from the start, been a fair fight. Although he didn't look it, the actor had been forged from premium ore, polished by tenacity, sweat, and grit.

A Jewish Russian immigrant at age three, with an unpronounceable, fifteen consonants, and vowels name, he grew up poor, hard, and tough on the mean streets of the New York's Lower East Side. He'd lettered in six varsity sports in high school, was a decorated veteran of WW II, and had once managed a gym, being expert enough a boxer to teach the sweet science to policemen as part of their self defense training.

Few are left who remember the momentous night. The Barn has long since succumbed to the developer's blade, the site, near the intersection of Davis Boulevard and US 41, now an auto repair shop. Scruff is a ghost in the fog of local folklore.

And the New York actor fella who whipped Scruff McGullis? His role on the TV series Tallahassee 7000 was the break he needed to make it to the big time. And hit the big time he did. After a career that lasted over fifty years, he remains one of our most beloved actors. A winner of the Academy Award, Golden Globe, and every other accolade Hollywood has to offer, his biographies always overlook one other achievement. The obscure yet absolute fact that at one time, long ago, in a small Florida town, he was the heavyweight champion. One Saturday night. At *The Barn*. This, rumpled, stooped- shoulder gentle giant with the wry smile, twinkle in his eye, and thunderous fists we remember as *Walter Matthau*.

ORKIN, COME QUICKLY Dave Dampier remembers this yarn. As he tells it: One early morning, after the bars had closed, we got an urgent call from The *Roach*--Royal--*Castle* that a fight was in progress in their elegant establishment. I arrived and entered to find a fellow down on top of Mr. Geek Splatt, a local thug, stool pigeon, and barfbag. He was applying a heavy fist quite forcefully to Mr. Splatt's head. I attempted to break them up, which I think Splatt would have been thankful for at that point. But, the combatant with the upper hand, or should I say fist, would not cease his rapid application of said fist.

We hadn't been carrying "Mace" on our belts long at that time but I quickly thought of it and did thereupon retrieve the canister from its new shiny holster and applied a healthy spray to the faces of both combatants. They immediately became disinterested in the manly arts, disengaged from each other, and began rubbing their eyes and crying like infants in need of a good burping.

This, however, was just the beginning. It was a rather warm and humid pre-dawn and the air conditioning system was trying hard to cool the building full of an after hours breakfast crowd. Too many bodies, too much air circulation, and a tad too much "Mace" precipitated a chaotic exodus. Even the hired help--cook and waitresses--abandoned the joint.

I even had a few tears myself--some from the Mace and some from laughing at how effectively the chemical spray had fumigated *The Roach Coach*.

JUDGE JOLLEY by MIKE GRIMM I was in Judge Jolley's courtroom in Everglades one time back in the 1950's, waiting for a traffic accident case that I was to testify in and enjoying the parade of cases prior to mine. In one, a man from Everglades had been hauled in for gambling and maintaining a gambling establishment.

Deputies testified that they were called on a noise complaint by a neighbor and upon investigation, found a large group of men in the defendant's house, shooting craps, drinking, shouting and generally having a good ol' time. When the deputies came in through the front door, the gamblers went out through the back door, windows, and a large hole in the floor, like rats deserting a busted bank . The only one they caught was the defendant, who had no where to run.

When it was the defendant's turn to testify he rendered the following tale: "Your honor, I was sitting peaceful on my front porch just minding my own business when this bunch of fellers came up and said they was gonna shoot some craps in my house. I protested and everything but they went on in anyhow. I was afraid if I made too much fuss they might mess me up, so I just sit on my porch and stay out of it. Then the deputies come and didn't ask or nothing but they come up on my porch and went right in the house and busted up the game. But they didn't catch nobody and they was pretty mad about that, so they arrested me. And I wasn't even in the game, your honor. I don't know a *thing* 'bout gamlin', and that's the truth."

Judge Jolley eyeballed the defendant for a minute without speaking. Then he smiled, looked him in the eye and asked, "How do you make a five *the hard way*?"

The defendant busted out laughing and declared; "Yes sir Judge, that's a good one."

Jolley banged his gavel and said, "Guilty! $35 or 30 days! Next case."

And *that's* the truth.

Editor's note: All you decent folks out there, who don't know about Craps, would have looked the Judge in the eye with a blank expression. Not so our defendant, who *knew* you *can't make a hard five* in Craps. Hard means the two die have the same number. Two threes equal a hard six. Two fours a hard eight.

AUBREY ROGERS The first time I met Aubrey, *and* Chuck Whidden, I was a civilian--having too much fun. Living at the time in one of the first Brookside Village homes, and working at the Tracking Station on Marco Island, we were throwing a house warming party. Or TGIF party. Or *whatever excuse we could come up with* party. It got pretty wild and I was not too surprised the next morning when Dep Rogers and Dep Whidden tapped on my door. The visit was not for what I had expected.

After confirming who I was and that there'd been a party there last night Aubrey asked, "Did anyone give you anything?"

Had to think on that a moment, then said, "Some folks contributed a few bottles of booze."

"Was any of it champagne?"

"Yep, it was," I said and it's still under the sink there. I won't touch the stuff, have a taste for Jim Beam."

"Mind if I look at it?" Aubrey said.

I told him sure, opened the cabinet and started to pick it up. He stopped me. "Let me," he said, "taking out his handkerchief and lifting the bottle from the very top. Just like Jack Webb did on TV. Caused me to wonder.

"We'll need to take this with us," Aubrey said.

And I said, "Whatever suits you tickles me to death." And that was the first time I met him.

Seems two of my guests, who I barely knew, had stolen the champagne from some rich guys house, a stupid thing to do in Mr Roger's territory.

Today, I'm thinking of the *last* time I saw Aubrey. We were at some department function, and Aubrey was already long retired. We, as old guys do, were talking about the old days.

"You know when I was driving in today," Aubrey said, "looking around at what a beautiful town we have, I remember all the things that went into the making of it by a lotta folks. And I like to think I was one of them. And that we did a pretty good job."

Correct on both counts old friend. A fitting epitaph and rich legacy you've left behind.

Aubrey Rogers. A true original. The likes of which will seldom pass this way again.

TOO MUCH OF A GOOD THING Years ago, along with the good the Civil Rights movement did, there was some attendant overkill. The liberal courts moved to the side of the criminals, with The Miranda Warning, and other asinine mandates that made our job much more difficult.

Included under the Civil Rights rulings, were provisos designed to halt the bad 'ol cops from picking on the poor, defenseless prisoners. After all, they hadn't done anything but rob, steal, rape, murder, and prey on decent folks.

Prisoners soon learned how to file a Civil Rights Violation against a cop, which could make them a little money, get the cop fired or jailed, and mitigate whatever slimy deed they'd perpetrated to get our attention. And, they were good at it.

We had an expert in our jail, who I'll call Terrance Turdbowl. Turdbowl decided he could use a big helping of that civil rights relief stuff and decided JD Spohn was just the man to serve it up. Every time JD would walk by his cell, he'd make a nasty comment. *Here comes fat ass. There's ol' sh-t for brains.* But JD, normally as volatile as Jake LaMotta, played it cool. Nothing worked until Turdbowl spit through the bars on JD. JD, immediately, opened the cell and gave him an open-hand slap across the mouth.

Turdbowl picked himself up, smiled, and said, "Now I've got your ass. I've got a dozen witnesses (other inmates) and I wanna use the phone to call the FBI."

Within a week, an Agent from the Miami office arrived to investigate the complaint. *Investigate* may not have been the proper verb. The FBI didn't like this crap any better than the cops and would help you *sweeten* your testimony. If you'd let them.

The Agent asked, "Sgt Spohn, didn't Turdbowl make some t*hreatening move* at you, causing you to defend yourself?"

"Nope," JD said. "Somebody spits on me I'll gonna jack their jaws."

"Perhaps you didn't understand me," the Agent said. "Did he made a *sudden move* at you that you thought was aggressive. . .?"

"No, I just give him what he deserved."

This went on for a while, until the Agent looked at me in

exasperation. I said, "Let me try. JD and I speak the same language." I turned to JD. "Either your damned memory improves or we're gonna be in deep Umpah!"

JD, surprised, stared at me a moment then the lights came on in the empty stadium. "Oh, yeah, I remember now. I went in there to council him, and he started to cock his right and I had to defend myself. Didn't want to hurt him, so I just gave him a little slap."

Everyone was happy--except Turdbowl--and the Agent returned to Miami, *No Cause For Complaint* form in hand.

Those times are long gone. Cops get a civil rights complaint filed against them today, they *are* in deep Umpah.

NIGHTMARE ALLEY Once I answered a call on 3rd Ave South, or one of those avenues near the beach that have an alley behind them. Several also had guest houses. This call was from a distraught lady who said she hadn't seen her guesthouse tenant for a whole day and *that just wasn't like him.*

It was dark when I arrived on scene. Spoke briefly with the complainant. She went on about how nice and reliable the man was, young, handsome, but seemingly unable to get over his recent divorce. She knew he was lonely because he came to her house each day for an afternoon cup of coffee. And he'd linger. But today, he hadn't shown up. She'd knocked on the door but no one'd answered. And *that just wasn't like him.* I asked her to give me her master key and we went back to the rental.

Walked around the house and tried to look in the windows but all the blinds had been pulled with not a sign of interior illumination. Finally, I pounded on the door several times, shouting, "Police, open up," with no success. Asking the landlord to wait outside, I used the master and opened the door.

It was dark as doom inside and when I tried the light switch nothing happened. (Found out later, he'd turned off the electric.) I flipped on my Ray-o-Vac and remembered it needed new batteries. The open front door wasn't affording much illumination from the streetlight outside so I decided to open blinds. (The windows, we later found, had been covered with blankets.)

Stumbling around in the dark I came to an abrupt stop when my face smacked up against something cold. . . and naked. I made a speedy retreat. Finally working up my courage, I re-entered the cottage, taking a different path, hands out, groping at the darkness until I found a window and ripped off the blanket. At that precise instance, the landlady, who'd followed me in, let out a blood chilling scream. I could see why.

In the tepid light, her tenant could be seen. Hanging by the neck, naked, from a light fixture. Gravity had been at work, his neck stretched and thin. Eyes bulged, imploring. A thick black tongue had pried open his mouth.

An unbearable sight for a lady to see. Or, I found after many a black-memory, terror-ridden sleep, a rookie cop either.

THE HOARDER'S WAREHOUSE   In the Industrial Park, near Domestic Ave, I found a treasure trove. Looking for a warehouse for the Sheriff's Office, I stumbled on the building by chance, noticing the doors open and a car parked outside a seemingly vacant property. Being a cop, I was nosey.

The warehouse belonged to an old gent that'd passed on and his family, living up North, was disposing of his property. When their agent opened it, however, their plans required a drastic re-evaluation. Inside were stored over 50 automobiles, none newer than about 1950. The vehicles, covered with an inch of dust, ranged from a Studebaker Champion to a Duesenberg luxury sedan. The family, before this discovery, had no idea what Grandpa had squirreled away in the building. They knew he was eccentric, but, hell at that age who isn't?

The cars weren't all. A large office area was full of his other collections. He had stacks of old comic books. Newspapers. The prizes that were given in cereals and *Cracker Jacks*. Toys in unopened boxes. Hundreds of plastic models, none opened or assembled. All this stuff piled so densely that you had to turn sideways and scoot through to trans-navigate the room.

I was told later that the family sold the whole works, sight unseen, to another collector for $100 K. Talk about bargains. You could almost hear the old hoarder spinning in his grave.

Oh, yeah. There was one other vehicle, sitting off to the side: a 1948 GMC pickup truck that had been owned by just one family since it was new. Being a pack rat of sorts myself, I bought that one for $1200 and drove it home.

EXPERT ADVICE Local governments love to hire consultants. At a staggering cost every year. Why? So when they want something they think the voters may not like they can blame it on the consultants. *We're just doing what the experts recommend.* Right!

Don't get me wrong, there are legitimate and needed consultants. We're talking about the ones who make a living *recommending* what the folks that hire them want. I worked with enough to know the difference.

The slick ones come to you and sniff around until they know what you're after. The blatant ones, don't waste time and, up front, ask what you want them to prove. It's a disgusting waste of tax dollars perpetrated by spineless politicians.

Once the City hired consultants to recommend changes in how we did things, intent on making the agency more efficient. Might have been a good idea if they hadn't hired dopes. For their 10K fee--a lot in the sixties--their final recommendation was to put men on the beach riding ATV's; a recommendation the City dropped in the trash can immediately.

And, some of their surveyors were suspect. Let Mike Grimm tell of his interview with one. The expert was using the Chief's office.

"When I got sent in there to be interviewed, he talked to me for a bit, enough that I could see he was in way over his head. Then he wanted to playact a hypothetical situation.

"He told me to go out in the hall and casually stroll through the door as if I were window shopping on the street. He would be a bad guy running out of the bank, with a bank money bag, right in front of me. He wanted me to react as if it were the real deal.

"So we did it, he bumped into me, I shoved him away, pretended to pull my piece and told him to freeze. He wasn't happy. I was supposed to be *off duty*, he said, and not carrying.

"He said we had to do it over and he was going to act like a *real* bad guy so I'd better act like I would if it were for real. I mumbled something about not wanting to hurt him and he took exception to it, saying I'd better worry first, about not getting hurt myself.

"So we did it again. I walked in through the door and he ran into me, hard. Kinda surprised me and I grabbed him, as much to keep my balance as anything. He started yelling and tried to twist away from me so I jacked his ass up and slammed him into a corner, immobilizing him. Then I stopped and he wanted to know what I would do next. I told him that in a real situation I'd put the cuffs on him. He told me to just try it and immediately started yelling again and thrashing around trying to get loose so I bent him over a two-drawer file cabinet and put the cuffs on him-- with just a little *extra* squeeze to try and get the point across.

"That was about the time you and someone else came busting into the room to see what was going on. Apparently he hadn't done this with any of the guys he had interviewed before me and it was a big surprise.

"As I recall, he didn't try it with anyone he interviewed after me either. He was one weird dude."

And an inept, stupid one. Mike was well over six-feet and 200 lbs. I remember when we rushed into the room, the *expert* was red-faced and gasping, his clothes disheveled, and his hair as mussed as a punk rocker's. Don't know what he was expecting but it sure wasn't Mike Grimm.

ORDERS IN THE COURT   Some of our transplanted cops had to deal with culture shock in other ways. Ray Barnett, a graduate of the Pennsylvania State Police Academy and alleged *Yankee* at the time, found the court system here more than a tad unusual.

We'll let Ray tell it: I was testifying about a stop sign violation case and said, "Mr Brown was traveling south on 10th Street and blew the stop sign at 12th Ave No." The Municipal Judge called an immediate recess and called Chief Sam Bass to the court. They took me out in the hallway and said, "we don't talk like that in court."

My immediate thought was I should have said *failed to stop*, not *blew*. Before I could explain, the Judge said, "You never call someone like *that*, 'Mr.'"

That meaning Mr Brown was a *black man*. The Judge and Chief then excused my transgression while I stood there with my mind reeling.

Never made that mistake again.

And that was my first impression of the judicial system in Naples.

Ray made few mistakes at anything but he did admit to one other. Again, in his words.

One I'll never forget is when I won an argument with a County Judge. In the dining room at the SO where we took our coffee breaks, the Judge said there was no such charge as drunkenness. I was dumb enough to go get a statue book, bring it into the dining room, and, in front of those in attendance, point it out to him.

Later that week he had me re-type a search warrant several times before he would sign it. That's when I learned it's not always good to be *right*. Especially when you're dealing with a super-ego Judge.

ROOFEES   The Naples Beach has always been a premier attraction. And long before we had shopping centers to attract auto burglars and assorted other thieves, the beach drew them like politicians to a lobbyist's *free* Caribbean cruise. But, let's face it, because of folk's disregard for security it was an easy way to make a slimy buck. How's that?

Ladies think if they put their purse on the floor and throw a towel or newspaper over it, the thief will *never* look there. Wrong, madam! That's the first place they *do* look because *everyone* does that. Of course there're many who are too lazy to even make that futile effort. *They leave it in plain view it the seat.* At least put the stuff in the trunk!

But, sometimes, even that didn't work. Then, each automobile manufacturer had just a few key combinations for all their models. We'd commonly catch thieves with an 8" ring of keys--a hundred or so--that would open a majority of American cars. General Motors used very few keys for their entire fleet. Chances were good your Chevy key would open your neighbor's Pontiac.

All thieves knew that and where to buy the key sets. They also knew you could buy spare lock cylinders *with* keys. Using a bent-straight paper clip inserted in the small hole beside the key slot, you could remove that one, insert your own cylinder, and drive off.

The best thieves didn't even need that stuff. On surveillance films we'd seen thieves approach a car, rock the window down a half-inch, drop through a string with a loop and a fishing weight on it, lift an interior lock button, and they were in. All in less than a minute.

Some thieves had homemade "Slim Jims" that, when slid between the window and door, opened the lock with just an easy tug on the interior mechanism. Or, there was a Ford model that you could hand-bump on the rear corner of the trunk and the trunk lid would magically open. Thank God all that has improved over the years. Now, if we could just get folks to lock the damn cars.

We had one cop, Byron Tomlinson, who had magical powers when it came to catching Auto B and E'ers. And everyone else. Byron could look down a beach-end avenue from a block away and catch the buggers in the act. Did it too many times to be explained by pure chance. The rest of us weren't that gifted.

Most of the activity took place at the Pier. The angle parking there, allowing the thief to get between two cars and not be seen, made it impossible for even Eagle-Eye Tomlinson to see them. You needed some elevation if you hoped to see anything. So, Mike Grimm, Ray Barnett and I took turns lying on the roof of the Price house, just south of the Pier entrance. The roof was made of copper. Directly in the sun. Even with cardboard, blankets, and camper mattresses, in about thirty-minutes we'd be medium rare--and we never caught a damn one.

Mike decided to try other roof tops but none had a good view. Finally, he climbed to the roof atop the three-story old Naples Hotel at the end of the avenue leading to the Pier. He was afforded an excellent view--of the palm trees that lined said street. Nothing else.

Eventually, I guess we aggravated them enough, and Byron and the other uniformed cops *caught* enough, that they'd go elsewhere. Most were from out-of-town.

But, they always returned, like the Snowbirds who fed them.

Choir Practice
Session Four

WINKIN' AND BLINKIN', FROM TOO MUCH DRINKIN'
Here's a great yarn from Dave Johnson. Dave's retired from the CCSO where he put in over 30 years. One of the youngest ever hired to the CCSO--attested to by the photo--he was still in high school when he became a Dispatcher-Jailer. He retired a Captain.

Late one midnight shift, Paul Canady and I were out on SR 92 near Goodland, parked on the roadside window to window shooting the breeze. I spy this little light, way down that long straight road. It's on for a minute or two, then off. On for a minute or two, then off, and so on. Pretty soon, along with the light, we can hear this whine coming from a motor. Every time the light would go off, the whine would stop.

Finally it dawned on us what it was. It was a drunk on a motor scooter. He was coming back from boozing it at Royal Palm Hammock, trying to get to Goodland before he turned into a pumpkin. He could hold it pretty good until he got up to 15 mph or so, then everything would go to hell and he would wreck. He had piled that scooter up at least 10 times before we finally got him corralled and saved him from a death of terminal road rash.

He was scraped up something awful, but was so full of "Who Hit John",--liquid stupid--he was under full anesthesia. We laughed so hard, I almost wet my trousers. But, we felt so sorry for him that there was no way we were going to charge him with anything--just took him to the ER and let them patch him up. I seem to remember him sobering up quite a bit once they started in all that raw skin with the scrubbies full of iodine......

Editor's note: Cops used to be allowed to exercise a little humanity, as was done in this case. Lawyers have killed that. Now, if the drunk you've taken home, stumbles and falls in the toilet you get sued. Cause you should have taken him to jail.

Consequently, if you get sloshed and stopped today you're going to the Graybar Hotel, no matter how pitiful your case. If the cop doesn't do it, he'll be in trouble.

And, we're still producing more lawyers than all the other countries in the world combined. And they have to do something. Hence, personal injury attorneys.

SLEASY WEASEL MECHANICS   A word of advice: Never have work done by a mechanic you don't know and trust. If you must, make him give you a signed estimate for services. If it goes over the estimate, he has to get your permission to proceed further. With the estimate in hand, he can't do what this sleazy weasel did.

A lady called that she was at a gas station on the trail close to Lake Park and needed help. We'll call it Maggot's Garage. The young lady had taken her Corvette in for a sweet deal tune up. I think about $25 bucks at the time. When she returned for the car, she found Maggot had disassembled the entire input system--carb, intake, fuel pump, the works--and wanted $200 before he would put it back together. He said the system was "dirty" and he'd had to clean it.

She didn't know the law and hadn't gotten an estimate. Moggot did know the law. He was one of those greasy rag mechanics you run into at some franchise brake and transmission shops. You take your car in for the advertised special, and no sooner get seated than here he comes out of the back, rubbing his hands on a greasy rag and shaking his head. "Shocks are gone," he'll say, or "cylinders ruined", whatever is the most convenient lie. He'll even show you the worn out hydraulic cylinders--that he's saved from another car. Or let you walk under the lift and look at the fluid dripping from your shocks. Fluid he's sprayed there with an oil can.

In the lady's case, we made Maggot an offer he couldn't refuse and he did the right thing. But sleazy weasel that he was, Maggot was soon at it again.

We'd had many complaints that folks had taken their car there to have the transmission fluid changed, and when they checked it, the fluid looked just like the old. So we put the ol' sting on Maggot, and had a civilian employee take a car through we'd doctored. When it was returned we checked and immediately took it back to him.

"Who says I didn't change that fluid?" Maggot raged. After we showed him the white, eggshell seal we'd placed on the drain plug, with my initials on it, he changed his tune, running to the back of the shop and yelling at a mechanic, "You rotten sonofabitch, what're you trying to pull?"

"Just did what you told me to do," the mechanic replied.

Maggot got to think that one over in jail and pay a hefty fine. But, after he got out, he was so reformed that he wrangled a lucrative City towing contract.

Kinda made us wanna put someone else in jail.

CHESTER'S UNIQUE MEDAL This is a unique photo in that it shows the presentation of a medal to a Naples Police Officer in the 1960's. Up to that time, there was never a medal given to any NPD cop. At least as far as we can determine. And there wasn't another for several years thereafter. Nowadays, with cop's shirts looking like a Latin-American dictator's, it's hard to believe. But that just wasn't one of the priorities back then. It should've been but wasn't. (Probably had to do with money, the cost of the medals)

Chester won this one by jumping in the water between a dock and a boat slamming up against it to rescue a gent who'd passed out and fallen in after enjoying too much--you guessed it--liquid stupid. Chester risked his own life to save that of another. About that time, for somereason, Gov Claude Kirk decided that cops were doing heroics around the state that should be recognized. He developed a one-time awards presentation to honor these brave souls. From police reports, Claudius Maximus picked out 16 officers and called them to Miami on July 16, 1968 for a Grand Awards Ceremony. Chester was one of those selected.

These were the only medals given and the only time. The mold was broken to insure that. Researching, we can find no evidence that any other Florida governor has repeated the act.

So, it was indeed an original. First and only of its kind for many years.

And richly deserved.

This shows Chester receiving the medal from Chief Sam Bass. The award was originally presented to Chester by Governor Claude Kirk.

THE GALLSTER HOLSTER George Gallstone was a cop with the Ft Myers PD. They'd been having some gambling trouble in a rough section of town called Dunbar, and George was assigned to work the area in plainclothes. See what he could turn up. George didn't like the assignment.

"Workin' over there by my damn-self at night, I could get beat up. Killed even."

"You've got a gun," his Sgt said. "If you're worried carry two. A knife. Whatever."

"That ain't the problem," George said.

"So. . ."

"They can jump you, knock you in the head. You don't have time to get your gun outta the holster."

The Sgt shook his head. "You'll figure out something. Just do it. Marked cars will cruise thru there regular, like they always do. We usually have someone workin' a complaint in that area, anyway. You'll be okay."

George was a good cop so, despite his misgivings, he followed orders and did his duty. Besides, he had an idea that gave him comfort.

Later that night, one of the patrol cops pulled up beside the Sgt's car, stopped at a traffic light. He was laughing so hard he could barely talk. "I was just over in Dunbar and I saw Gallstone sneakin' around. You ain't gonna believe it. Go take a look."

The Sgt drove to Dunbar and found Gallstone lurking in an alley. He had something in his hand. A first he thought he was carrying a brown, lunch bag. On closer inspection, he could see that Gallstone's hand was inside the bag. He drove by George and told him to meet him around the corner, out of sight.

At a safe distance away from Dunbar he asked, "Just what in hell is that on your hand?"

"Little invention of mine," Gallstone said. He loosened the rubber bands he'd rigged to hold the bag in place, dropped it away, revealing his hand, gripping a revolver. "Never get the jump on me now," he said.

Most of our embarrassing acts of stupidity--thank God--are swept away on the tide of time. Others, become legend. To his dying day, whenever George Gallstone met a Ft Myers cop he was asked, "Hey, George, still usin' that Gallster Holster?"

NO FEAR HERE   Soon, my body will succumb to a lifetime of neglect and abuse and malfunction, making me a menace behind the wheel. Then I'll hear mumbled conversations behind my back--by my children--trying to figure out how to get the car keys away from me. But, I ain't worried. Here's why.

Once received a call from a friend named Bert in Port Royal. Bert asked if I could come down and see him. Said there was some urgency. He'd meet me outside his house on Galleon Drive. Arrived and saw Bert, waving me to the curb. He rushed over and jumped in my car. After greeting him, I asked the problem.

"It's Dad," he said. "He's 93 now and insists on driving. And he. . .well, if you have a few minutes you'll see. He drives down to the clubhouse every morning about this time. Gotta get his startup toddy. He. . ." --stopping, looking at the house,then--". . .here he comes now."

A stooped, frail, ancient dude emerged from the front door. Maybe emerged is too active a verb. Snailed through would be more descriptive. He inched along like a mummy with the gout. It took him ten minutes to negotiate the distance between his front door and the Lincoln in his driveway. Short sessions of hobbling along, were interrupted with rest stops, leaning on his cane. I didn't think he was going to make it. But he did.

At the car, he struggled to get the door open, then slowly folded himself into the seat. Seated, he began lifting his legs, with his hands, over the desired pedals. It was obvious this old gent shouldn't be allowed at the controls of a hospital bed.

"See what I'm talking about?" my friend said. "We've tried to convince him he needs to give up the car but he won't hear of it. Say's he has a perfect driving record and if he ever has an accident, he'll quit then."

"Common problem," I said.

"But, he's going to kill himself, or someone else."

"Think I can help," I said. "They have a new law allowing cops to request a re-examination of suspect drivers. Cases just like this. You get me his DL number and I'll call it in."

"Okay," Bert said, "I'll get it this afternoon when the toddies put him to sleep."

He was good to his word and I made the arrangements for the re-test.

A month later, Bert called again. "What the hell kind of operation are they running down there?" he said.

"Why," I asked.

"He got the notice, went down there, and passed the damn test."

And he had! I inquired of the examiner how the hell that could happen.

"The State's always making these new rules, rules that we don't have the money or time to implement. So we just give them an eye test, no driving. Most old folks fail that. But, your guy had eyes like an eagle.

"And the body and reflexes of King Tut," I said, disgusted.

But, the problem solved itself a couple of weeks later. Tutankhamen got in his car in the garage, put it in backwards, and drove through the partition between his garage and kitchen, killing his dishwasher, range, and a nifty Ronco Veg-O-Matic.

So, getting old? What me worry? I had my cataracts taken off two years ago.

TERRIBLE THOM Part One-- Being a cop, you find that monsters come in all sizes. I was investigating an attempted arson of a boat on Central Avenue. The boat was on a trailer in the carport and someone had spread newspapers under the boat and a can of gasoline was sitting nearby. The victim said he'd seen the visiting kid next door out in his carport. I went next door.

His name was Thom and he was six-years-old. Visiting, with his mother, from up north. As handsome a youngin' as you'd ever see.

"Were you next door trying to set that boat on fire?" I asked.

"Why do you think it was me?" he asked, with no more trepidation than Charley Manson.

"There was a witness," I lied.

"Well, then," he said, unconcerned, "you've got me."

I was stunned at his candor. "Why were you gonna to do that?"

"I asked the old son-of-a-bitch to take me for a ride. He said he was too busy. Old bastard's retired. Too busy! So I figured if he wasn't going to use the damn boat, I'd just burn it up."

And that was it. No remorse, No fear. No nothin'.

"Who saw me?" he asked

"No one," I said, "I just said that."

He smiled. "You're about a tricky bastard, aren't you? I like that."

Again, not what you'd hear from a child. That was just the beginning.

Thom read the newspaper each morning. Beginning with the front page all the way through. He preferred the Miami Herald, calling the Naples Daily News a provincial gossip sheet. Again, he was six-years-old. He also read Time and other magazines you wouldn't expect. His vocabulary was much more extensive than mine. In everything besides size and age, he was a brilliant adult. I decided to do some checking on his home ground.

Thom wasn't any stranger to his hometown cops. Indeed, he was the main suspect in the death of his grandmother. After peeing Thom off one day, someone had spread newspapers all over her kitchen, soaked them with gasoline, and set fire to the house. With her in it.

They'd suspected him and given him a psychological eval. That didn't work too well. About half-through, they figured out that Thom was manipulating his responses to make fools out of them. Playing with them. They said his IQ was off the chart.

The cops couldn't prove Thom had burned up his granny. When they questioned him, he asked what would happen to the person who killed her. When he found out the police took such shenanigans seriously, he clammed up.

I guessed he didn't think burning a boat was that big a deal, since he'd fessed up so easily. I gradually found out, he had a psychopathic personality that excused anything he did.

TERRIBLE THOM Part Two-- Terrible Thom was scheduled for Juvenile Court for his attempted arson. Judge Richard "Wretched" Stanley presiding. Since Thom was a visitor and due to go back up North, some exotic and completely illegal and unenforceable transfer of the case to his home state had been arranged.

Thom was seated at the defense table with his mother, and I at the prosecution table, when the chamber door burst open and in charged Judge Stanley, scowl on his face and black robes flowing like the Wicked Witch's from the West.

Suddenly, Thom was at my side, grabbing my hand. "Can I hold your hand, Detective Young?" he said. "I'm really quite terrified of the Judge." And at that moment he wasn't the miniature monster but just a scared six-year-old kid. And I felt so sorry for him.

Thom survived the court hearing, hand in mine, and returned to Yankeeland. About a year later, I received a call from the detective

I'd talked to before about Thom. He had news. It seems Thom had gotten into an argument with his mother and struggled with her. The basement door had been left open and mama slipped and fell down the stairs, breaking her neck and killing her.

"I just know this little turd shoved her down those stairs but the case is thin. 'Course it's juvenile court and, with his background, not much evidence will be needed."

"So what'll happen?" I said.

"At most they'll lock him up until he's eighteen. Then he'll be released, a full grown psychopath, to do whatever he wishes."

"Hope he doesn't come South for the winter," I said.

Over the years I lost track of Thom. But, rest assured he is--and thousands of others--out there. With names like Ted Bundy. Dahmer. Gacy. Ridgway.

FLYING SAUCER--OPEN CASE We've written about explained UFOs. Here's one that was never accounted for. It was first told to me by the Crime Scene Tech at the CCSO, Marvin Mayo, who took the case photos. I've since been told the tale by many other Deputy witnesses.

On March 14, 1965 a local rancher was camping, with his passel of hunting dogs, in the Everglades. Night had fallen and all was quiet when his dogs became agitated, doing the things dogs do when they sense something's wrong.

Then a pulsating light, that seemed to be drifting towards earth, suddenly appeared. He estimated that it was about a mile away and suspected it was an aircraft in trouble. Thinking he might be able to help, he fired up his swamp buggy and headed in the direction of the brilliant light.

As he approached the spot where the "plane" seemed to have gone down, he found no wreckage, only a circular, cone-shaped object emitting pulsating light. The craft was about 75 feet in diameter and 30 feet tall. It was hovering slightly above the ground, emitting a humming noise and wobbling like it was trying to keep its balance. The were several rows of ports in the side from which a yellow light radiated.

The rancher stepped down from his buggy and approached on

foot. He didn't get far. A thin blue beam rifled from the craft and slammed him between the eyes. He was immediately knocked unconscious.

When he awakened, though stunned and half-blind, he was able to make it to his buggy and limp to the hospital. Examination revealed a large red spot between his eyes, blurred vision, and atrophy of his muscles. His eyes seemed to have suffered from X-ray.

Investigators at the scene found no space craft but evidence that something strange had been there. A large circle was scorched in the foliage and the tops of the trees burned out. Mayo said he didn't know how any human could've burned, or controlled the burn of such a perfect circle. And there was a strange smell coming from the earth.

The US Air Force invested UFO sightings at the time and they were called to the scene. They were notorious for ridiculing the sightings, but in this case were reluctant to. The rancher wasn't the usual nutty, glassy-eyed sighting witness. He was an established, well regarded citizen. Then there were his physical injuries that he couldn't have inflicted himself.

The bottom line was an official report was never issued and the case languished until it was forgotten. Except by those who'd been there and seen the victim and the eerie burned circle in the Glades.

THE GAME TABLE MAN   Dave Dampier remembers an early morning scuffle at the Royal Castle.

Says Dave: I heard a call to the R.C. dispatched to one of our officers, a behemoth nicknamed "The Surfer." This epithet had been earned for several embarrassing incidents, all involving driving police cars on the beach, wet sucking beach sand, and feverish wrecker calls to avoid vehicle submersion.

The Surfer was already inside when I arrived. And, a confrontation with a combative subject was in progress.

I'd just entered, to assist The Surfer, when I saw him unload on the fool who'd decided to fight this giant of a policeman. The combatant seemed to spin in midair and return to his prior position, causing the officer to thump him again. Then, another spin and return.

When the subject was restrained and the situation under control, I could see what had caused him to react like one of the little men on a hockey game table when the rod is spun. The subject had backed up to the "cattle guide" brass railing that keeps customers in order when approaching the counter. When punched, he spun backwards over and around the railing, returning to his starting position in front of The Surfer. Thinking the subject was still showing aggression, our man would send him spinning again.

I know it was far from funny to the spinning punching bag but, as far as a comedy act The Three Stooges couldn't have done it better.

CLOSE ENCOUNTERS OF THE LIQUID STUPID KIND

It was after 3 AM and we were in the PD having a cup of jailhouse battery acid. The bars had closed at 2 and we thought we'd put all the drunks to bed.

All except one. We heard him before we saw him--a thud just like a vehicle makes when it hits a tree. We ran to the window and looked outside. A man, who'd obviously enjoyed too much liquid stupid, was running from a pick-em-up that had jumped the parking space and used a palm tree for a stop bar. He was looking skyward, with his arms folded over his head like he was warding off a sea gull umpah bombing. We met him at the front door.

He rushed right by, squeezed in a corner of the lobby and muttered. "Flying saucer. . .chased me. . .bright lights." We tried to calm him but it took several minutes to get his story.

He'd been drinking near Royal Palm Hammock, and when the bar closed, got in his truck and headed up US 41 to Naples. He hadn't gone but a mile or so when a bright light focused on him from overhead. Nearly blinded, he drove on, increasing his speed, trying to get away. But he couldn't outrun the light.

"It chased me all the way to town, then disappeared," he said. "I knew you guys would be open so I came here."

We knew a UFO was unlikely but knew how objects in the night sky can be misread. A few months before I'd see a blazing, bright light overhead that suddenly took off and disappeared over the horizon. UFO? Looked like it to me. But a call to Cape Canaveral dispelled that notion. It had been an aluminum weather balloon, over New England, up so high tomorrow's sun was shining on the aluminum. When it reached a certain altitude, the balloon popped and fell to earth. From that height and distance, it look like it was streaking away across the night sky.

About that time, the phone rang, the dispatcher talked a few minutes, then smiled and handed the phone to me. It was an officer for the game commission.

"Just wanted to let you know," he said, "we were running poacher patrol tonight and checked out a dude on the East Trail. Driving a pickup truck from The Hammock to Naples. Think we scared the pee-water outta him. He took off like a French soldier. We dropped off when we got to the city. You might run into him somewhere."

Mystery solved. The game commission, at night, would fly over trucks coming out of remote areas and check what they were carrying in the bed. Looking for a dead deer, other poached game. They flew in a helicopter--with a very bright light. Probably not the smartest way to do business, but it went on for a while.

We tried to explain to our visitor what had happened but he wanted none of it. "Was a flying saucer. Tryin' to get me in their space ship so they could probe me. I ain't stupid."

We gave him a chance to reconsider while he sobered up in the jail, and had his truck towed out of our front yard.

ENDANGERED GATOR This is one of the original Alligator Alley mile marker signs. They were an instant sensation and proved to be so popular they were stolen as fast as they were erected. Or replaced.

They were also used for target practice by idiots with both a car and a firearm. Note the .22 cal hole at the top of the sign.

The State finally gave up and replaced them all with the standard, un-cool variety mile marker signs. Problem solved but a lotta smiles lost along the way.

And no I didn't steal this one. It's a photo, from Chester Keene, of a stolen one seized by the NPD years ago.

My *personal* sign disappeared a long time back. Probably some A-hole stole it.

SHARK TALES There was a period when shark fishing was a big deal at the Naples Pier. Before that, and I presume now, folks that wanted to grapple with Jaws would lay outside Doctor's or Gordon's Pass on the outgoing tide, and try go catch the monsters where they naturally congregated. Sharks like to do their fishing in spots like that, being garbage collectors of any trash food the tide washed out.

But, for some reason, a few fishermen thought it was a real good idea to lure sharks to the Pier. And they did. Any evening you'd see these dubious sportsmen with monster rigs, baiting up with rotten hams, roasts, or fish parts and slinging the mess into the Gulf. Some even used chum, pouring buckets of putrid fish guts into the water. And at least once, most nights, the bait was taken and a fight commenced.

Sharks don't willingly give up the life/death struggle. The fisherman could fight the beast for hours, being dragged up and down the Pier, crossing everyone's lines, and disrupting all the other fisher-folks fun. And when the shark was finally landed, the battle was still not over.

Once a nine-foot Hammerhead was hooked, battled for hours, and eventually dragged up on the beach. When the fisherman walked up to his prize, thinking it was dead, he was greeted by a, suddenly, very alive Hammerhead slashing and trying to play some catchup. The fisherman decided he'd better call the cops and let them deal with the monster--that wasn't much fun now. Sgt J.D. Spohn arrived.

Spohn nudged the shark with his toe, and when the critter came to life again, took out his revolver and put six thirty-eights in the shark's head. That just made Jaws angrier so Spohn, never outgunned, went to his patrol car for heavier artillery. He returned with an M1 semi-auto carbine and went to work on the shark with that. Content the job was done, and it being after midnight, he left the carcass on the beach to be removed in the morning. In the AM the hammerhead was still alive.

Scenes like this caused some sensible council folks to decide that maybe luring these formidable killers to an area where people liked to wade and splash about in the surf, wasn't such a real good idea after all. And shark fishing from the Pier was curtailed.

Smart move. During the same period we had an early morning swimmer disappear and his body never recovered.

THE SELF-INDUCED COMA There's no doubt that booze, liquid stupid, is responsible for many of the jaw-dropping situations a cop encounters. It's as reliable as canned laughter on an unfunny sitcom. Mike Grimm remembers one such occasion:

While on patrol late one night, Jack Bliss turned off U.S.41 and headed East on 17th Ave No. to check out a pair of slow moving, weaving tail lights. He pulled the car over and found inside two of Naples' most reliable drunks--who we'll call Boscoe Putter and YeeHaw Bunion. Boscoe was at the wheel.

Jack bagged them up along with a quart whiskey bottle that was less than half full. As was protocol at the time, Jack marked the level of the whiskey in the bottle before putting it in the evidence room, which in those days was a closet that didn't even have a working lock on the door. (Some cops carried evidence around in the trunk of their car until it was court time)

On court day, Boscoe appeared and brought YeeHaw along as a witness for the defense. The only problem was, YeeHaw was nearly as drunk as he was the night of the arrest.

While being questioned by the City Prosecutor, Yeehaw had to keep jerking himself awake as he mumbled and gave incoherent answers to most of the questions. Finally, in exasperation, the attorney tried to pin YeeHaw down to answering one simple question concerning Briscoe's condition the night of the arrest.

"Tell me" begged the prosecutor, "what was Mr. Putter's condition that night when the officer pulled you over? Was he sober? Was he a little tipsy? Was he in a coma?"

At that, YeeHaw's head jerked up and he was suddenly very lucid.

"Hell no", he shouted, "he wasn't in no coma! We was in a Ford Falcon station wagon!"

Everyone seated behind the bar, including the prosecutor and the judge, suddenly spun their chairs around to hide their laughter from those in the courtroom audience.

Fortunately for YeeHaw, Judge Tom Brown-- a kindly man--did not charge him with contempt of court for showing up drunk to testify. Good laughs are sometimes hard to find in a courtroom.

BURRITO ON THE PIER John Slater was much better at collecting animals than he was corralling them. He'd turned his estate, on Gordon Drive, into a sanctuary for exotic animals. He was so caring he had food, from their indigenous area, flown in every day. Nothing was too good for the dolphins, giant tortoise, wallaby, and other critters. Yep, he was good at collecting but he just couldn't build good fences. Or, as some suspected, he thought it was funny to let some critters escape and wander the preposterously pompous neighborhood.

One jail breaker in particular, called Pedro, was known to anyone who visited the City Pier. He was a mini burro who loved to mingle with the fishermen. We regularly got calls, from folks concerned about his safety, that the little fella was on the pier.

Chester Keene received such a call one day and found the burro in the midst of some fishermen, soaking up their adoration. It was obvious to Chester that there were a million ways Pedro could get injured. First, and most likely, the fishermen were notorious for not being particular where the hook end of their line was when they cast. Just flip it over their shoulder and give it a fling. Doing so, they hooked pelicans, birds, and humans and a jackass wasn't beyond reason. Then, Chester reasoned, Pedro could fall off the pier. Or get his hoof caught in the planking. Yep, he needed to go home.

There was a short rope around Pedro's neck--formerly a tether-- and Chester tugged on it. And tugged. The little burro just stood there as though his feet were nailed to the deck. That went on for some time, with the fishermen enjoying the show, and Chester, not wanting to hurt the burro by jerking too hard, getting more and more frustrated.

Finally, one of the fishermen had mercy and told Chester the problem.

"Never seen you out here to capture the burro before?" the fisherman said.

"Nope," Chester admitted, it was his first burro wrangling detail.

"Well," the fisherman said, "what he wants is to jump off the pier."

Chester looked hard at the fisherman.

"Really," the fisherman said. "He likes to jump off the pier and swim to shore. That rail over there," the fisherman said, pointing at the bait house, "is made to come loose so they can pull up the bait nets. We take it down and he jumps right in."

Chester thought he was being had, and only after repeated assurances let the fishermen demonstrate. One unscrewed the wing-nuts that held the rail in place and moved it to the side. The burro immediately ran to the opening and jumped into the Gulf. And swam like Tarzan to shore. Once there, he walked up on the beach, shook himself like a soggy dog, and headed south on the sand towards home.

Wonder what's next? Chester thought as he went 10-8. Big John's Galapagos Tortoise gonna take up water skiing?

PS Besides being a tasty treat a *burrito* is Spanish for a small burro.

ANYTHING'S POSSIBLE On the phone, I could hear the excitement in Sarah's voice. "Wait'll you see what I've got!" she said. Sarah was Sarah Creamer. At the time, she and Dave Johnson were helping me hire folks for the Sheriff's Office. And it was hard, often unrewarding work.

We were trying to hire about 100 a year, Civilian and LEO's. The cops were particularly tough to find. I know that some of you out there, who've seen in the news media some of the stupid things cops can do, won't believe it but the requirements are so narrow and stringent that only about one of every hundred we talked to were selected.

It's the old Marine Corps rule of thumb, sorta like the Bell Curve. You can make every test available, give them physical and psychological evaluations, written exams, background investigations, and still, about 10%, when they come to work, will turn out to be turnips. Of course, the ol' Curve works on both ends.

Ten-percent will be geniuses--nearly as troubling as turnips. But 80%, thank God, will be the regular, normal crowd that make every organization run.

Howsumever, Sarah's excitement got my blood up, too. She evidently had one of those rarest of the rare, an applicant, that on first sight you just knew was a keeper. And he was working, already certified, no academy required. "Bring 'em on back," I said and went to the office door to greet the prize.

He was moving down the hall in a measured step, a big youngin', clean-cut, warm smile, when he saw me waiting.

"Howdy," he said, shaking my hand in a vice grip. I ushered him in and pointed to a chair. He sat, and I started to begin my spiel. But he beat me to it.

"I expect your time's valuable," he said, "so I'll get right to it. Does your department require a physical agility test?"

"Yep," I said, "state law to get certified. Didn't you take one where you're working now." (It was up around Arcadia)

"I passed it once, but I'm not sure I could do it again."

"Why's that?" I asked, "you look healthy to me."

"I passed it before they cut my legs off."

I knew he was too good to be true, I thought. A wiseass. I'd seen him walk down the hall and there wasn't a hint of a limp.

"It's true," he said, reading my mind. "Got T-boned on duty. Had to take both my legs off, one at the knee, one above the ankle. To prove it, he lifted his trouser legs and showed me. And yep, there were two plastic things under there.

"But," I saw you walk in," I said, "not even a slight limp."

"Doctor's said I'd never walk again and it made me mad. I'm a stubborn guy and don't like to be told what I'm not capable of. So I went back to work on the desk, and practiced until I could walk normally and could work on the street again."

"But, you can't run?"

"Well," he said, "I can but it's not my best thing. Sometimes I loose my balance. I won't take up any more of your time he said," getting up.

I walked him out to the front lobby and told him I was sorry it didn't work out. And I was.

He eschewed the elevator and walked down the two-story staircase to the front door. Nary a wobble.

Standing there watching him march away, I had to wonder what things we all could do if someone hadn't told us they were impossible.

BUT YOU SAID. . . Another tale from the memory of Chester Keene.

It was a slow night and the two young dispatchers were fighting terminal boredom. To keep awake, they were inventing games, telling jokes, doing anything to stay on the flip-side of Zzzzland. They were right in the middle of a Charades session when in walked the dreaded Chief of Police. He was a retired Army Colonel and liked to drop by, unexpected at night, and try to catch someone goofing off.

Tonight, he had to be ecstatic. His tirade was maniacal and brutal, concluding with, "You might as well put on a couple of dunce hats."

Please keep in mind that this was a pair of rookie dispatchers, who knew little of The Colonel, except that he was known for making strange requests and was roundly despised by the cops. So, to improve their performance, and try to make the Chief happy. . .

The next night the Chief was again doing his weasel patrol and drove by the front door to the PD, then at 8th and 8th South. It was glass and he could see the front desk. And what was visible behind the counter--two cone-shaped hats. Bursting in the office, he got the full effect: the two busy dispatchers, wearing homemade caps with the word DUNCE printed on each one. Just as he, sarcastically, had demanded. We always believed it was one of the things that led him to consuming too much liquid stupid and, consequently, a six-month tenure as Chief.

A few years later, Saturday Night Live featured a recurring skit called The Coneheads. I wonder. . .

ARCHIE AND THE PEEPING TOM One of Naples' early mayors was so colorful a book could be devoted to his shenanigans.

His name was Archie Turner, a fisherman turned to snagging voters. And he was excellent at it. Archie was a physically powerful man, even though he had one arm that'd been mangled in some sort of accident. It hadn't slowed him down much. He was also a Bataan Death March survivor. Tough guy.

I remember once, at the Swamp Buggy Races, the drivers decided they were going to throw Archie in the Sippy Hole, the biggest and deepest hole in front of the grandstands. Just good ol' fun and games for the event and times. Archie threw six of them in the hole before a mob could overpower him and give him a dunking.

Another time we received a call that there'd been a prowler at Archie's house-- on Central, about three blocks up from the beach-- looking in his daughter's window. We rushed to the scene and found an agitated Archie, saying the bastard had run, and pointing in a direction. I took off that way.

Along the route, I came upon an old gray Chevy sedan, lights out, idling beside the road, with the driver hunched over--trying to make himself invisible. When he realized I was the police, he was terrified and admitted he was waiting for his partner, who was the peeping tom.

I yanked him out of the car, handcuffed him to a stop sign, and decided to finish his duties. Taking off and cruising slowly with the lights off, I hadn't gone far before out of a yard burst his compadre, who ran to the side of the car and jumped in. "Where the hell you been?" he said, before looking at me and realizing he'd been tricked.

When we arrived at Archie's, he ran up to the car--blood in his eye--tore open the door, grabbed the voyeur, and lifted him arms length in the air, with one hand on the kids neck. "If you ever come back to my house again and look in my daughter's window," he said, "I'll break your scrawny neck."

He certainly seemed sincere to me. And to the kid, too. He had some extra laundry to do down at the jail.

SPEEDY VS LURCH One of our Dets, Ken Ferrell, was a good cop. And a karate master. And a lover of unusual pets. In the Detective's office, where he worked, he had a terrarium set up. Anytime you walked by you'd see some new--and usually frightening--critter he'd acquired. To Ferrell, lizards, snakes, things most of us thought repulsive, were as cuddly as a baby kitten. Once he even had a tarantula named Lurch.

Ken would let the hairy monster, as big a teacup, walk all over him. And he tried to get others to share a little quality time with the beast, too. Most like me, would like to see how much shoe the thing could hold up with a 230 lb cop standing in it.

Feeding days, Ken would capture a big palmetto bug, or several lesser nasties and throw them in the terrarium. Lurch would come instantly alive, stalking the meal until he'd trap it in a corner, then one leap and it was chow time.

One day Ken came in with a new tasty treat: a chameleon. The chameleon we named Speedy Gonzales. The little fella wasn't but about two inches long and we figured he was dead lizard walking.

When Speedy was dropped into the terrarium, he looked around, saw his adversary, and stood dead still. No good. The spider made an immediate rush for the snack and  gave his signature leap. And landed on nothing. Speedy was using his suction-cup feet to hang safely out of reach, up on the glass wall.

Lurch looked at the lizard a few minutes, then turned his back to walk off. Just what Speedy was waiting for.

He leaped from the wall on Lurch's back, and did a most violent Mexican hat dance--stomping, kicking, biting--until Lurch fell to the floor in confusion and exhaustion. And Speedy returned to the glass wall.

This cycle went on all day. Lurch would recover, stand up, and Speedy would do another fandango on the bedraggled hide.

The next morning, when the office was opened, Lurch was laying on the terrarium floor, eight legs in the air, stoney dead. And Speedy was scouting around the cage, looking for his own tasty treats.

"Damn," Ken said, " I paid good money for that thing." Then, being Ferrell, he shook his head, smiled and said, "Guess I should've given him some karate lessons."

DON'T FENCE ME IN This is another true yarn from Chester Keene.

Received a call requesting to see the Shift Supervisor ref a problem that needed reconciliation. The Request for Supervisor usually means a cop has stepped on someone's toes, and they want to whine and blubber and get a second opinion as to what the cop had said they'd done wrong. Or they're just those particular jerks who believe they're above the law--in Naples, at the time, common place. Neither of which was so in this case.

Found the complainant, and elderly woman, in her front yard. She said that she needed help with her husband, who was in the backyard. Asked if he needed medical attention and she replied, "Not yet, but if he keeps it up he's going to."

In the back yard found her husband, standing in the hot sun, peeping through a privacy fence.

"Looks okay to me," I told the lady.

"Yes, " she said, "but if he doesn't get out of that hot sun, get something to eat or drink. . .he's been there almost all day."

"What's he looking at?" I said, having a pretty good idea.

"Go take a look, you'll see."

So I did. I greeted the husband at the fence, told him why I was there. His eyes looked like rotten grapes and his breath sputtered in ragged, irregular burps. "Need to take a look through that fence," I said. The geezer reluctantly stepped aside, took one last look, then relinquished his spy-hole. I took it over.

On the other side, laying topless beside the pool, were two lovely spring-breakers. Early twenties at the most.

In the cop business you're always doing things you don't want to do, but it's a duty thing. So I took one last look then announced: "This is the police. Put your tops on and quit exposing yourselves." The young ladies quickly complied.

The keen observer at my side mumbled, "Damn," and sulked all the way over to his wife. His wife said "Thank, you," to me, and I got in my patrol car and returned to duty, marveling at her reserve and understanding.

A sunstroke averted, a marriage saved, and life went on in the treacherous Elephant's Graveyard.

Choir Practice
Session Five

DELIVERANCE FOLK The Hillbillies in our East Tennessee town of Bashful Beaver lived exclusively in a section we called *Deliverance*--after the Burt Reynolds movie. Cops seldom received a call from Deliverance since Hillbillies don't recognize the law. Or law enforcement officers. You could talk to one and they'd look right through you, never saying a word.

We did, however, receive many calls *about* Deliverance. Hillbillies take care of their own problems so we'd get calls from mail carriers, delivery folks, and such, that there was a body lying beside the road or shots had been fired. One sad afternoon I was assigned such a call.

"Some woman's screamin' like she's being slaughtered", the UPS driver said. By the time I got to the reported address, all that could be heard was a loud TV.

The "residence" was really just a shack, no bigger than a two-car garage, hammered out of rough-cut lumber. The front door was standing open. Inside were three rooms: One bedroom, a kitchen and the living room. The floors were linoleum rolled over packed-down dirt. Out back was an outhouse and a nearby well.

There were ten people sitting on the floor—no furniture. No one acknowledged my presence, all transfixed on the TV. At the time, large screen TV's had just come out. They were a contraption where the front folded out and projected an image on a background. And they were very expensive. This is what the Hillbillies were watching, the latest technology resting incongruously on the linoleum and dirt floor. God only knows where they stole it.

The critters themselves were typical Deliverance folks. There's something about inbreeding that causes genetic horrors, head shapes that are "lumpy", distorted. The heads look like they were fashioned in clay, then smashed until the skull was no longer symmetrical and one squinty eye's an inch higher than the other. The kid playing the banjo in the *Deliverance* film is typical of this unmistakable

Hillbilly marker.

I said, "Howdy." No one answered, nor would they ever. So I looked around.

On the rear step, outside the kitchen, I found where the screams had emanated from. Blood was everywhere. It indeed appeared that someone or something had been slaughtered. I called for an Investigator and watched *Gomer Pyle* reruns on the monster TV until he arrived.

The Investigator, Burly Hardcase, arrived shortly, appraised the scene and said, "Lets look around the house, curtilage for the body-- which we ain't gonna find. Been here before, fights between one of them lump-heads and his sister/wife. Knew it'd come to this eventually."

"What then?" I asked.

"Nuthin'," Burly said. Didn't see him or her in there by the TV. I'm sure he's out in the boondocks burying her right now. Forget about asking them," he nodded toward the TV crowd. "No one in there'd piss on ya if your skivvies were on fire. So, if we don't find anything, we move on, write it off."

I couldn't believe it. "Move on?. . ."

"Yep," nuthin' else to do. Besides it has a good side. That's one less sow to be squirtin' out these lop-headed defects. And that ain't a bad thing."

I've thought about his pragmatic solution many times. In retrospect, Burly may've been right.

MORE'N ONE WAY TO SQUASH A ROACH   Years ago, when I worked a short time for the Sheriff in Bashful Beaver, where we now vacation in Tennessee, I had to learn some unique concepts. These extra-legal tactics *did* make the job easier but I kept thinking of the day when I'd no longer be a cop and at the mercy of systems like this.

One of the things overlooked, I found out, was extradition. The Sheriff called me into his office one day and said he was sending me out of state to pickup some prisoners.

"Three of 'em, take lottsa chain. And a cattle prod." he said.

"What'd they do?"

"Just got outta Brushy Mount, so naturally they got plastered, stole a car, and wrecked it."

"Whereabouts?"

"Down there in Georgia," he said, "little town 'bout fifteen miles south of the Tennessee line. Chatsworth."

I knew the place. "Who has the extradition papers? They already down there?"

"*Extradition papers?* " the Sheriff laughed. "Hell you don't need no extradition papers. It's just in Georgia."

"But. . ."

"We have an *understanding*," he said. "No problem."

Dubious, but having seen several other expediencies that were "no problem", I gassed up my cruiser and headed south. In less than an hour I was parked in front of Chatsworth's small but beautiful stone courthouse. Inside, I told the friendly receptionist my business, she made a call, and soon I was met by a Chatsworth PD officer. We'll call him Marty Multitasker.

"These Aholes have about as much brains as a dingle-berry," he laughed. "Driver passed out and forgot to take his foot offa the accelerator. Scruffed 'em up pretty good. They ain't gonna be no problem."

"I might have one," I said. "Don't have any extradition papers."

"No problem," he said. "Besides, who they gonna complain to? Guess they could call the *Mayor.* But that's me. Or the *Municipal Judge*. But that's me, too."

And he was! Corporal on the PD, Mayor, and Municipal Judge.

Now you see why we say *The South's gonna rise again*. Don't take near as many folks to run the government. And there's not all that worry over laws and stuff, either.

HAPPY HOMEMAKER'S HINT An article in a recent law enforcement journal extols the virtues of using *wasp and hornet spray* to ward off human pests. It claimed that hornet spray, which will shoot a stream over 20', is much better than pepper-based sprays that require you to be up close and vulnerable. And the effect is just as, if not more, devastating—probably requiring emergency room attention. And a hornet spray can is innocuous, requires no permits, and is safe—on the user's end. Readers were encouraged to put one in their glove compartment and beside their bed.

The article caused me to wonder just how effective hornet spray would be. Sounded reasonable. Being at our summer place in the Great State of Tennessee afforded the ideal proving ground. Cops in the county, where we vacation, are not bashful about experimenting with new procedures and devices that inflict pain and misery. In fairness, they have to, to deal with the sub-human hillbillies in the community who are, on the evolutionary scale, two generations below the cast of *Jersey Shore*.

I consulted with some members of the local constabulary who I knew. The reaction was unanimous. *Hornet spray! Why didn't I think of that?* They agreed to test the proposition in the field and report the results. By the very next morning, I was listening to a report by an enthusiastic experimenter.

"Shoulda seen 'im," the Bubba Cop said. "Know how when you spray one of them hornets they fall right to the ground, and starts kickin' and floppin' around?"

"Yep," I said.

"Well," he said, "a hillbilly does the same damn thing 'cept *better*."

"How's that?"

"*A hornet can't scream.* Hell, I've turned in my Capstun and bought me a case of Black Flag."

I offer this report for your perusal, edification, and consideration. Hopefully, It'll assist you in product selection. Just remember that in todays litigation prone society using the spray might be a quick trip to a long civil trial. But me, I'm cuttin' this short so I can get down to the bug section of the hardware store.

JAYMAR'S STIMULUS PACKAGE J. Marshall Humpyall--"just call me JayMar"--was gonna have a real busy Thursday. And Friday. There was the house to buy. The new car. And, of course, the Chris-Craft yacht. He began the day early at Ambiance Realty, *Palaces for the Obscenely Rich*. He met with *Mr Ambience* himself, Oilkan Slipp.

Oilkan looked across his desk at the middle-aged man in gaudy golf attire and tasseled-loafers. A clone of all his customers requiring *comfortable lodgings* in Naples.

After three hours in Port Royal, JayMar had selected a waterfront beauty and given Oilkan some earnest money with instructions to proceed. By the end of the day he'd acquired a Cadillac convertible and a boat big enough to boogie down to Bogota on.

Friday, just before noon, he was in the old Bank of Naples, on 5th and 8th South, seated with the New Accounts VP. The VP's presence was warranted by the size of the check JayMar had presented to open the account: a cashiers check for about 200k, drawn on a bank in the Bahama's. This was big money in the late 60's.

"I'm going to need a little walkin' around money," JayMar said.

"No problem," Mr VP said, "how much?"

"Oh, I'm going to need some furniture, some new clothes. . .twenty thousand should do it."

Taken aback, Mr VP said, "Of course, but with a new account, that size withdrawal, and the check being from out of the country, we're going to have to verify it. Policy, all that."

"No problem," JayMar said. "Mind if I smoke a cigar while I wait?" Not waiting, he produced a big bucks *Montecristo* Cuban cigar.

Soon a clerk came to the VP's desk and relayed hushed info to the boss. When she left, the VP said. "We can't verify the check until Monday, the banks in the Bahamas close at noon on Friday."

"Oh, goodness," JayMar said, "what am I to do? I've just relocated here, and the house I bought today won't be ready for at least two weeks, so I'll need lodging . . . and money."

Mr VP's ears perked up. "You bought a house?"

"Yes," JayMar said, "a place in Port Royal."

"How nice."

"And a new car. And a yacht. I'm not some fly-by-nighter. You're welcome to call and verify the purchases if you'd like."

And so the VP, greedy for the account called. The realtor. *Yes, he bought a fine home on Galleon Drive. Lots of ambience.* The car dealer. *Baby blue convert, just like Elvis drives.* The yacht dealer. *Yes indeed, a nice 40 footer.*

71

"I believe that should be satisfactory," Mr VP said. "We'll make that advance."

JayMar smiled, and took a big drag of his *fake* Montecristo.

When Monday came and the bank in the Bahama's said the check was bogus, JayMar was long gone, waiting for Thursday, so he could work his magic elsewhere.

You see he hadn't really bought or taken delivery of anything. He'd made *down payments* on the house, car, and boat--with bum checks on the same bank in the Bahamas. That couldn't be cashed--or verified--until Monday.

It was a bitter pill for the hometown bank, but the taste had already left their mouth a year later when they fell for the same scam perpetrated by a "dentist" retiring to Naples from the islands.

GOT YOUR NUMBER Thirty-some years ago someone came up with a good idea. It was called *Operation Identification.* If that sounds familiar it's because it's still in use today. A national program, all law enforcement agencies were urged to join and promote it locally.

The idea was you engraved a number on valuables that would be likely targets for thieves. The number would be registered with the local police. Then, when the thief tried to pawn the item, or sell it on the street, the prospective buyer, seeing that it was identifiable, would be reluctant to purchase same. And if the thief got caught with the item, there'd be some heavy-duty splainin' to do.

Folks who wanted to participate were loaned an electric engraver, shown how to use it, and instructed to scratch the number on the property to be protected. Today, the number is usually a two-letter designator for the state, then their driver's license number. When their property has been marked and the their personal number registered with the police, they are given stickers to put on their home to warn thieves they should look elsewhere.

The program was very successful. In little 'ol Naples hundreds of citizens participated in the program and branded their goods. Trouble was, the number we prompted them to use back then is the number they are warned to *never* give public exposure today. That's right, their *Social Security* number.

Back then, it was a logical number to use. Highly individual, no two the same. Best of all, the scams that are dominate today had yet to be developed. Fortunately, most of the gear marked with the SS number is no longer in use.

Just a reflection on how times change. And not always in the right direction.

JUDGE, GET OUTTA MY CAR Once a Detective in Ft Myers, who thought he had a "slam dunk" case against an auto thief, was stunned when the judge dumped the charges and set the maggot free. The judge, who we'll call Stinkweed, told the Detective, who'll be Wiley, that the thief had a title to the "alleged" stolen vehicle. And it was true. "But, your honor," Wiley said, "it's a *bogus title*, obtained by fraudulent means. And we intend to prove it." "No need," Stinkweed said, "a title is a title as far as I'm concerned. Too complicated to sort out. Case dismissed." Wiley was distraught, but not destroyed. He decided it was time to educate the Honorable Stinkweed, who had about as much business on the bench as Homer Simpson. Immediately before being appointed a judge, he'd served a period of disbarment for stealing his client's money. About a month later, Wiley, entered Stinkweed's chambers and said, "That blue Caddy Coupe de Ville you've been driving. . ."

"Yes," Stinkweed said, "what about it?"

"It's my car," Wiley said, "and I want it back."

"What the hell are you talking about?" Stinkweed thundered.

Wiley handed his honor a piece of paper. "Here's the title, with my name on it and the VIN number matches that Caddy."

"It can't," Stinkweed said, befuddled.

"But it does. You see I called up a motor vehicles department in some backwoods county in Alabama. Gave them them the VIN number off your car, gave them my name, and a bogus address in Alabama, and told them I wanted to title a car I'd put together out of junk parts. Had them forward the title to me down here. Had it in about a week. Took that to a Florida DMV office, and converted it to a Florida title. Just like the thieving sonofabitch did that you released."

"So," Wiley continued, I'd like my Caddy cause as you said '*a title is a title'."*

Wiley, of course, didn't take the car, but his point was well taken. At the time *anyone* could get *any* type of title in Alabama, few questions asked. It was nearly as popular a shady enterprise as our camera-generated *right on red* traffic citations.

HANG 'EM HIGH In 1972, when the Supreme Court took all the fun out of the death penalty by declaring it "cruel and unusual punishment" a couple of local *hanging judges* took exception.

Judge Lamar Rose, by throwing a rope with a noose at one end over the limb of an oak at the Lee County Courthouse, aptly declared what he thought of the ruling. (That historic oak is the one they've recently cut down.)

At home here in Collier, Judge Richard "Retched" Stanley had shown and said what he thought of the death penalty beforehand. According to news reports, during the Porter murder trial, Stanley brought out the brass knuckles and pistol he carried and displayed them prominently before him on the bench.

At the time of the trial, when asked if he could personally execute anyone he said, "Well, I'll go along with that as long as they allow me, right after I pronounce the sentence, to reach down by my left leg and come up with my pistol, and shoot 'em right between the eyes."

The Porter jury didn't agree with the Judge and voted, unanimously, for a life sentence. Stanley ignored them and imposed the death penalty.

Later, the Judge's court clerk testified that even before the trial Stanley had told him that he was going to send the S.O.B. to the electric chair.

I knew Judge Stanley professionally and personally, having been with him at many social gatherings. And for his honor to leave the slightest bit of doubt where he stood, would have been way out of character.

And, he was usually right!

BYRON TOMLINSON Behind the old NPD, at 8th and 8th South, was the City Building and water tower. To the right of that,

74

an alley. Beside the alley was a small cottage where Byron Tomlinson and his family lived. We knew Byron well from the time he was just a youngster. A mischievous youngster. We used to joke that we hired Byron as a Dispatcher so we could keep a closer eye on him.

Gail Addison, who graduated with Byron, reminded me that he was the first Eagle mascot at Naples High School. Yep, that was him inside the Evil Eye Fleegle costume. He was also the vendor of portable *Screwdrivers*, oranges that he injected with vodka and sold to the other students. And he liked to put bumper stickers on my detective's car that read, "*This is an unmarked Batmobile.*" Once he even got the locked car open and put a Batman sticker on my steering wheel.

But, the fact was he was hired because someone saw in him a trait that can't be taught. He had that "right place at the right time" gene that would put him, magically, in the center of the action. Or the chase, or whatever was going on.

Chester Keene sent me a news clipping relating how Byron had caught two different groups of auto burglars on his *first two days at work* as a cop.

Byron was the first I remember to be allowed to become a cop under the age of 21. The age was lowered to 18. Trouble was we had to buy his bullets. You still couldn't buy them until you were 21.

Byron moved on to the CCSO where he was a Road Deputy, Investigator, and Lt in charge of the Marco Island Sub-station for years. Then, he started feeling bad.

Local doctors couldn't determine what he had and mis-diagnosed him a dozen times. Finally, a doctor/relative urged him to go to Shands find out what was pulling him down.

I remember standing out in front of the SO, smoking a cigarette, when Byron came walking up, just back from his Shands visit.

"What'd they find out I?" I asked.

"Said I had a disease called amy-something and I had 6-months to live."

I was floored. I knew he wasn't up to par but he was still young and looked strong and healthy. I thought he was putting me on.

"Don't worry," I said, "only the good die young."

He was dead in three months.

The disease was Acute Amyloidosis. Doctors don't know what causes it. As I understand it, your internal organs just start growing, then fail. At the same time, the Governor of Pennsylvania had the same thing and had transplants of his lungs and liver. But, it was only a temporary remedy.

Byron left another *Byron* he'd be proud of. He works for the CCSO and looks and sounds like Dad.

Wish Byron was still around to see it.

WIND ACROSS THE EVERGLADES In the late 1950's Everglades City was host to Hollywood. A major film, *Wind Across The Everglades,* was in production. Stars included Burl Ives, Gypsy Rose Lee, Peter Falk, and Christopher Plummer. Other's with small roles were clown Emmett Kelly and heavyweight boxer Tony Galento. And, there were bit parts for local's Chief Cory Osceola and Constable Joe Hunter.

Mike Gideon, retired CCSO Deputy, lived there then and said the filming and Hollywood crowd were a unique and fascinating divergence for the fishing village folks.

He remembers that Burl Ives, a man of generous proportions, wore long-handle underwear as part of his costume. Mike and the other youngins loved wash day when the huge long Johns were displayed on the clothes line. Mike said they were as big as the sail on the Santa Maria.

And that Peter Falk slept quite often on his screened-in porch. He said Falk, later TV's *Columbo*, was painfully shy. He *did* like to play chess with Mike and showed young Mr Gideon several moves.

But Mike said everyone's favorite was Gypsy Rose Lee. Gypsy had arrived in Everglades in a maroon and black Rolls with 28 cats. She took two rooms at the Rod and Gun Club. One for her and one for her cats. Or so it is said in news reports. Mike said he remembers her having two Afghan hounds, but no cats.

Mike lived upstairs over the Youth Center. The inside had been converted to *Wardrobe* and the porches *Make-up*. He said you could tell when Gypsy arrived each morning as her loud and friendly voice soon had everyone laughing at her jokes.

Burl had one other small problem. His character "Cottonmouth" carried one of the critters around in his pocket. Trouble was Burl was terrified of snakes. Even movie snakes that just *looked like* cottonmouths. Those were always interesting scenes to film.

MORE WIND Mike Grimm remembers that about a year before the film crew moved into Everglades to start that film, WNOG started the talk show, *Pub Time*. It was broadcast from the *Pub Room* of *Yeaman's Old Cove* restaurant. Pappy Grimm was the original host of the show. (Pappy Grimm was Mike's father)

When Gypsy Rose Lee came to town she agreed to be a guest on the show but Pappy had to go down there and tape it. No problem, until he got there. It seems that someone else was always demanding her time and he couldn't get a word in edgewise.

Finally she took pity on him, loaded him up in the back of that Rolls and had the driver go for a spin while they did the interview.

He was very impressed and became one of her best fans. Talked about it for years.

* * *

Scenes from *Wind Across the Everglades* were filmed at Smallwood's General Store. Now a National Historic Site. Mrs Smallwood had a bit part in the film.

* * *

Editor's note: *Pub Time* was a mainstay on Naples radio for years. It later moved to the *Piccadilly Pub* and was hosted by Bill Ryan, who became one of the owners of Palmer Broadcasting, that later became the present Comcast.

And, when the above picture of Gypsy was taken, she was considered to be the epitome of feminine pulchritude. No starvation diet there.

THE JOB My old friend and associate Dave Johnson sent me this e-mail: *Thirty-something years ago, I joined Collier SO. In those days, you almost couldn't give the jobs away. Poor pay and mediocre benefits. I was an 18 year old wet-nose, still 3 weeks from graduating High School and they hired me anyway! My nickname was "Pampers", which were a novelty then. I remember my dad almost kicking my ass for taking a job as a Deputy. He knew what real life had in store for me.*

How funny it is today that jobs with CCSO are all but unobtainable--much coveted for the decent salary and outstanding benefits--but no damn money to hire anyone with! Hundreds of applicants in stand-by mode. Government jobs are now the cream of the crop--a complete turn from the early 70's when you were one grade below washroom attendant.

His missive caused me to ponder. When I joined the NPD it cost me $100 a week in salary. I was working in the missile industry on Project Mercury. But I hated the work, wanted to be a cop.

Of course, money went a lot further back then. We bought one of the model homes in the *new* Brookside Village. It was $9,995. But, we couldn't scrape up the $300 down payment and had to take a second mortgage. Yep, the money went further, but not nearly far enough.

Chester Keene sent me his first pay stub from the NPD. He started on June 4, 1965 and was paid, for two six-day weeks, $166.62. That's gross, net was about $150. See why there weren't many takers?

Now, as Dave mentioned, Gail Addison, who was Personnel Director for the CCSO, says the lines are long and the competition fierce for the jobs. Incidentally, Gale was really the Human

Resources Director but I can't say that name without thinking of the movie *Soylent Green* wherein people were turned into food. Or, human resources.

DARK BLUE CHEVY II When I made Detective--about the time Sherlock Holmes did--at the NPD you wore a certain "uniform." *Business attire,* it was called. A suit, or sport coat with white shirt and tie. And you drove a stripped down Chevy, or Dodge, or Plymouth. Fords, back then, never seemed to win the car bid. It had black-wall tires and, with its yellow *City* tag, looked just like the low-bid unmarked police car it was.

Used to make me wonder why I just didn't wear a uniform and drive a marked car. Everyone knew who you were anyway. So I lobbied to make some changes. Finally, Chief Sam Bass gave in and allowed me to put out bids on something a little different.

Something different, turned out to be a dark blue Chevy II with white wall tires and a healthy 327 engine. Fitted with an out-of-state tag no one suspected who we were. (The other part of "we" was Mike Grimm)

Getting the car ordered required a little extra work. Casey Ingram, the local Chevrolet dealer, didn't want to order it. Said he didn't think it would be safe. Casey was like that. If some young person, with a lotta money, walked in and ordered a souped up Corvette, Casey would run them off if he thought they were irresponsible and might get killed in the car. We finally got Casey to give in by ordering the heavy duty suspension, available for police cars, that he insisted on.

Getting the uniform part relaxed took a while longer but I finally got that changed too so that we could wear sport shirts, untucked, to cover the gun and badge.

The little Chevy with the big motor would put about 7 G's on you when you accelerated. It was the fastest cop car in the county, except for maybe cars built by CCSO Deputy Charlie Sanders. Charlie was an ex-NASCAR driver and built police car engines, usually 427 Chevy's. And they would clock!

Howsumever, the NPD had a practice that the "Hoot Owl" shift, who crept around most of the night at low speed, would "blow out" their cars each morning before turning them over to the Day shift.

79

That meant give it a healthy run to blow out the carbon buildup. This was done on the road that later became part of the Golden Gate Parkway, between Goodlette and Airport Road. You had to be careful doing the blow out because the last quarter of the road was gravel, and made stopping an exciting proposition.

Many mornings we had *unsanctioned* drag races on this road, pitting one police car against another. Needless to say, the little Chevy II would blow the doors off any regular Impala and Plymouth Fury police car.

We kept the little car beyond normal trade in time, but eventually had to give it up.

I still miss it.

RUBBA, DUB, DUB Some days you wonder why you got out of bed. Newly, a CCSO Deputy, could tell you all about it.

The day started with great prospects. He'd just completed six-weeks of training with a Field Training Officer (FTO) after graduating from a lengthy Police Academy. Today was to be his first day on the job, *on his own.*

After completing the required paperwork, Newly was issued a patrol car; his very own. His first chore was to give it a through cleaning so he proceeded to a drive-thru automatic car wash to get the job done. He signed off on the CCSO account, and proceeded to the wash entrance. There were several signs posted along the way warning customers to roll up their windows and remove any magnetic signs, antennas, and the like. For some reason he didn't think the warnings applied to him.

Newly placed the car over the pull-thru track and soon a gentle tug told him he was underway. He watched contentedly as the water, then soap, then monster roller-brush crept up the front of the patrol car. Then over the windshield. Then--*Great Blubberin' Glenn Beck, what was that?*--a jerking stop and start and a banging on the roof like a cat-o-nine-tails was at work. But that wasn't the worst.

Next, the rear window exploded inward, the car was filled with water, liquid wax, and soap suds and Newly was floating in an upholstered bath tub.

When he was rescued, the problem was evident. The roller brush had made it over the light bar but caught on the heavy base-loaded antenna. This was ripped from the roof, whipped around the roller--causing the beating sound on the roof--then slapped through the rear window, knocking it out and letting the liquid mess in.

Poor Newly survived the incident and the day but had some heavy 'splainin' to do why he didn't read those signs.

Thanks to Chester Keene for *his* excellent memory and for jogging *mine*.

THE FRUSTRATION STATION The garage-looking building, south of the old Airport entrance on Radio Road that housed the Civil Air Patrol, was once the last place in Naples you wanted to visit. That was when it was the Vehicle Inspection Station.

This was where you went to get the required windshield sticker showing your vehicle was safe to be on the road. It was also where you dealt with unbelievable bureaucracy and incompetence.

Like what? Suppose you had a small car. You knew that even if it was straight from the factory it would fail the brake test. *Always.* The test required you to roll over a steel pressure sensitive plate and slam on your brakes. Invariably, the machine'd report your brakes were worn out and you'd *fail the test.* So, to get around it, you loaded the back seat with three of your friends and returned to the station. The extra weight would change the reading, endorsing your wonderful brakes.

Then, you had to unload your passengers before you took the headlight test. The extra weight in the back seat would cause your headlights to aim too high and you'd *fail the test.*

Folks dreaded the annual debacle. Some more than others. Our Lt JD Spohn was one of those who'd rather kiss Whoopi Goldberg than get inspected. Every year when he took his well-maintained Caddy for the check-up it failed. Then one day he had enough.

Having returned to the station after two trips to his mechanic for headlight adjustments--that the mechanic said it didn't need--and other bogus deficiencies, JD was livid when he finally finished the test. When the inspector started to reach into the car to scrape off his old sticker and install the new, JD said, "Nope, don't you stick your head inside my car."

"But how am I gonna see to put on the sticker?" the inspector whined.

"You figure it out. Just don't put your head inside my car."

"This is ridiculous," the inspector said, poking his head inside JD's car. Bad mistake! JD rolled the electric window up on his neck. And wouldn't roll it down. And started to drive away.

After a frantic call to the PD, we arrived and were able to calm JD down. And the strangle-ee, who was "gonna press charges."

"Go ahead," we told him. "JD will ask for a jury trial and no juror in Collier County, who owns a car, will convict him." The point was well taken and JD walked.

Shortly thereafter, with a *frog strangler* of complaints raining down on the state legislature, the stations were all inspected. It was found in ours that the machine that read headlight focus had *never been calibrated* since it'd been installed. *Never*. And the brake machine was about as accurate as the clowns who calculated Obama's budget.

It wasn't long before the stations were closed and the program sent to *Bad Idea Hell* where it belonged.

The program was based on BS to begin with. The idea came from accident reports wherein drivers claimed, when they didn't stop, that their brakes were defective. Of course they were lying but that's where the program emanated. Some bean-counter reading the data concluded that most of the cars in accidents in Florida had bad brakes.

Now you know how laws get made. Scary, isn't it?

MORE LIDS THAN THE MAD HATTER Over the years, the NPD has worn more lids than the *Mad Hatter.* It started with the traditional cop's 8-point, military style hat. Pretty standard for "city" cops. Later, we lost our way.

Someone decided that the hat style *Deputies* wore was the way to go. You know, the one Jackie Gleason's Sheriff Buford wore. The kind Lyndon Johnson might wear on Saturday night visit to a whorehouse.

They looked ridiculous! They were hot and itchy in the sun. To ward off rain, a plastic cover was necessary or they got soaked and

drooped down like wilted lettuce on a day-old Whopper. Nobody wore the damn things--although you were supposed to. But that was just the beginning.

When the country started having race riots, the NPD fielded a Riot Squad. Not a bad idea to be prepared. At the same time cops switched from using the short "billie" club to the longer riot stick. That was because newsies loved to film the cops, with the billie in the air, getting ready to crack some deserving maggot's

skull. It was easy to spot the billies raised above the crowd, a beacon for photographers.

The riot baton, however, was used in a *thrust and parry* fashion, poking ribs, cracking jaws, but not raised overhead affording Kodak moments.

All this made perfect sense. Then came the problem. Cops also wore a riot helmet. Again, some genius decided that the helmets should be worn *all the time,* while on duty. Now, we're talking about something like a motorcycle helmet. Hot, heavy, and blocking your normal hearing, they were also too tall for lengthy cops to wear when seated in a car. Damn things hit the roof, making you tilt your head forward. But a good cop can always figure out how to thwart absurd bureaucracy.

Soon you'd see cops riding or walking along with their heads appearing to *bobble* like one of those little dolls. The reason why was they'd stripped all gut's out and it was now just a thin plastic shell, balanced on the top of their head. Weightless and useless.

Finally, even the most dense administrator saw the stupidity and futility of the helmet rule. Especially since, in the Elephant's Graveyard, there was only one riot--*ever*--and that was in Immokalee.

Later, Riot Squads lost out to SWAT teams. SWAT dudes, in their black Ninja uniforms and masks and enough weapons to give a redneck wet dreams, were much more intimidating. And that was the bottom line to begin with wasn't it?

THINGS THAT GO BUMP ON THE BEACH Chester Keene reminds us of this one. Just like today, in the 60's, when you worked as a cop, there was never enough money to make ends meet. And every time you got close, some SOB *moved the ends*. So most of us took extra jobs, many in security, guarding construction sites on the North side of Doctor's Pass. This was due to trouble they were having, at the time, with unions trying to cause work stoppages. Then there were the material thefts always attendant on construction sites.

There was also a problem with turtle poachers on the beach. These A-holes would cruise the Gulf at night, close to the shoreline, using a spot light to identify turtle drag trails from the water to the weeds. Knowing the turtle would eventually return to the water after laying and burying her eggs, the scumbags would lay in wait, butchering the tired and near-helpless female at water's edge, leaving no evidence.

The Marine Patrol took counter-measures. They modified a patrol car, with a monster Ford Interceptor engine, by enlarging the wheel wells. Then they installed high-flotation airplane tires so they could navigate the soft sugar sand without getting sucked in. With this vehicle they could patrol the beach and outrun any puke they encountered in a jeep or 4-wheel drive.

One night, when Chester was finished with his extra security job, one of the Marine Officers named Blanco asked him if he'd like to take a ride in the souped-up beach buggy up to Clam Pass and back. Chester said he would and they took off through the sugar sand, the wide, half-inflated tires doing a perfect job.

About a quarter-mile north of the Seagate Beach Club, they came upon what looked like the remains of a sand castle someone had built. Blanco said, "look at this," and ran right over it. They were shocked when a loud scream resonated from the sand pile.

Chester and Blanco, quickly stopped and exited the vehicle where they found a young man crawling out of the pile. Amazingly, the man--obviously a Hippie--wasn't hurt. In fact, he said he barely felt it, but the surprise and engine noise "scared the hell" outta him.

When asked what he was doing there he said his companions were camped over in the mangrove area that is now Pelican Bay. He'd gotten tired, but the crowd was so noisy he went to the beach to get some sleep. There, he covered himself with beach sand to keep the no-see-ums off him.

Insuring the Hippie was unhurt, Blanco told him to get on the front fender and he'd return him to his camp. There, the Hippies were so disappointed at seeing the police, the party ended, they struck their tents, and headed for always sleeze-bag friendly Ft. Myers Beach.

No poachers were caught that night but the future Pelican Bay area was cleansed of the dreaded Hippies so that, cherished amenities intact, it would be fit for the future exclusive use of the rich and shameless.

Choir Practice
Session Six

NEW LOOK AT NAPLES POLICE DEPARTMENT includes four new patrolmen. Standing from left are C.H. Dasher, Kenneth Mullings, Chester C. Keene and Barry L. Kee. Seated are Jack Bliss, newly appointed acting lieutenant and assistant chief, and Acting Chief D.L. Bass. Freeman D. Wood, newly appointed police officer was not present for photograph.   (BURLINGAME- McGRATH PHOTO)

Changes at the NPD in June of 1965 Chief Ben Caruthers had moved on to Hillsborough County and the new, acting *Chief Sam Bass is shown with Jack Bliss, new Assistant Chief. Standing are new patrolmen C. H. Dasher, Ken Mulling, Chester Keene, and Barry Kee.* Not in photo is another new cop, *Bud Wood.* As you can see, back then large cops were preferred.

This is when cops wore white shirts in the summer and long-sleeve gray in the winter.

And, the *Collier County News* was now a daily, all eight pages.

WHO NEEDS WD-40? This story is from my son Wayde, who's a Deputy with the CCSO. And, there's some irony here. As told by Wayde:

Investigators in East Naples had received numerous reports of petit theft from *Long John Silvers*. It appears that several containers of new and used cooking oil were missing from the fast food restaurant. On further inspection, the investigators found that the thefts coincided with the working days of one particular employee. And cops hate coincidence.

When investigators couldn't reach the suspect by phone for an interview, they went to his place of residence--a weekly rental at a sleazy motel in the Naples Manor area.

Once they arrived there was no response at the door so the detectives gained access to the room through the motel manager. Inside the room they couldn't believe what they'd found. Several empty containers of cooking oil were strewn about. From top to bottom, the walls were plastered with nude *Playboy* centerfolds and pornographic "beaver shots"--photos from *Hustler, Penthouse* and other pervert's home companion magazines.

On closer inspection, the walls were slathered with the cooking oil making them extremely slippery. When the suspect was finally caught and interviewed he claimed he needed the oil because he liked to get nude and slip and slide around the room. Turned him on. Made his, uh, *libido* so hard a cat couldn't scratch it.

Now for the irony. Over forty years ago we, at the NPD, had a case so similar it's eerie. When we got to the suspect's rental room we found he'd covered the bed with plastic sheets and greased it with cooking oil so he could slide around while fantasizing about the centerfolds on the walls.

And just like the CCSO cops, we tagged this perv with a handle that has endured through the ages. Yep, you guessed it, *The Crisco Kid.*

MONSTER IN THE NETS This yarn from Chester Keene. As he tells it:

A commercial fisherman was tending his net off Keewaydin Island's beach. Waiting for the tide to change, he watched the net line, illuminated by a small electric light attached to a boom. The light was just just bright enough to see, but not too bright to scare away the fish.

When he was sure the time was right, he started pulling his net over the stern roller, the dim light allowing him to see the catch coming into the boat.

All of a sudden, he started to get resistance on the float line. He would pull, it would pull back until it stalled. Finally, after getting the net going again, he was startled when out of the murky shadows lunged from his net an ugly dark creature with bright white teeth.

Not knowing what it was, in defense he picked up a boat oar and struck at the beast, and connected with a thud. The swing's arc also knocked out his meager light . After getting it functioning again, he could see the critter on the beach and could tell it was a chimpanzee. It was obviously the one that ran free on the island, raising havoc on many occasions.

The fisherman's last view of his net-crawler was the ape stumbling up the beach, his hand on his aching head as if he'd had a bad night at the *sand bar.*

Editor's note: This chimp was a notorious villain. The property of the island's owner Lester Norris, the chimp had gotten mean with age--as is common with the species.

Mr Norris used to let the NPD hold parties on Keewaydin and at one the chimp, who was in a cage, grabbed the arm of my son Wayde, and bit right through it. The only way I could get him loose from my son was to gouge my thumb in the beast's eye.

This works well with reluctant humans, also.

THE LONG ROPE COLLECTION AGENCY At one time you could hire a collection agency that pretty much guaranteed you'd get your owed money. It was started by the Hell's Angels. When ten of them showed up on a slow-payer's doorstep, with their leather-studded hand out, you'd better put something in it. Naples had a short-lived enterprise that also worked well.

A very successful construction subcontractor, who we'll call Frank, was excellent at completing projects on time. Except for one element: his bookkeeping skills were so terrible he was constantly writing bad paychecks to his employees. It wasn't that he didn't have the money, he was just awful at accounting for it. Didn't send out bills on time. Didn't collect them. Forgot to make deposits. He loved to build but hated the paperwork. And he didn't have a bookkeeper.

Payday was always a hassle for Frank's employees. A waiting and worrying game. Who would be the lucky ones to get a valid paycheck. All? Half? They just never knew.

You'd think they'd give him up to the cops for uttering rubber instruments, but he provided steady work and paid better than anyone else. When he *did* pay. And the workers knew Frank *would* pay. Eventually. He was just sloppy at getting it done on time.

One Friday afternoon we received a call from Frank's receptionist--who wasn't a bookkeeper either. She was terrified. "You better get over here quick. Frank hasn't showed up with the checks and the guys are so mad they've strung up a rope with a noose back there in the shop. And I believe they're gonna use it."

We urged her to try and contact Frank and tell him to stay away until we could get there. She said she had and Frank was coming in anyway.

When we got there, we found just what the receptionist had described. The noose, the angry crowd, everything but a horse with Frank on it, hands tied behind his back.

Just as we were moving in to disperse the crowd, in walks Frank. There was a fearsome growl from the workers.

Frank smiled. "Sorry I'm late, fellers, but I got behind and have to admit I didn't have time to write out the checks."

Oh my God.

"But, I did bring cash money--he held up a brief case--so we can settle up."

And nothing can bring on the smiles like cash money.

Frank wasn't a stupid man and the incident brought a profound change to his monetary practices. After that, Frank's paychecks were as reliable as the afternoon shower on a Florida summer's day.

At least for a month or so.

The next time Frank's employees started to uncoil rope and fashion a noose, he decided it was time to hire a bookkeeper. We'll call her Gwendolyn.

He was well beyond the time his booming business should've had one anyway. So far behind that, after giving Gwen a few weeks to organize his financial mess, he asked her if he had enough money to buy a new car. And was shocked at her answer.

Gwen looked at him incredulously. "You're kidding," she replied.

"Well, I can wait. . "

"Frank," she said, "you really don't know do you?"

"Know what?"

"With all the lots you've been buying with your real estate pal, and your business proceeds, you're a millionaire. Easily." (Over the years, he was to lose this million, then make it back)

Frank happily bumbled on for a few more years. Then, he gave me a call. "I think I have a problem with Gwendolyn. I think she may be stealing from me."

I wondered how he would ever have known, given his aversion to things mathematical.

"Had an IRS audit, had to call in a tax attorney. He told me I may have an internal problem. He showed my books to another accountant and it looks like Gwen has skimmed off 100K or more."

I talked to the tax lawyer, he showed me what he had and I went to Frank's office. When confronted, Gwen easily fessed up. She said, over the years, she'd been short because of personal financial emergencies and taken a little here, a little there. She didn't realize it'd been so much.

I told Gwen and Frank that the amount constituted a felony, maybe prison time. Frank said he wanted to think it over before he decided what to do. The next day he called me up.

"I've been thinking about Gwen," he said, "and I remembered I *loaned* her that money. She didn't steal it."

"Come on, Frank," I said.

"Yep, actually I *gave* it to her as a bonus," Frank said, "yeah, a bonus. She's been so good over the years, keeping me outta trouble and all. Hell, she's saved me more than 100K."

"You sure," I said.

"Yep, that's my story and I'm stickin' to it."

And he did. I guess Gwen worked there until she retired.

Frank was very generous in other areas, too. For years he anonymously was one of the main financial supporters of PAL. We couldn't have survived without him.

THE MAGIC WORDS   So some Puke has broken into your house and you've shot them or stabbed them or cracked their skull with a 12" cast iron skillet and the perp is sprawled on your floor, in disrepair or, better still, permanently removed from the A-hole pool. So what now? First, call your lawyer then remember *The Magic Words*.

What are *The Magic Words*? A pronouncement, that when uttered correctly, helps defend against criminal charges or civil action proceeding against you.

This is what they *ain't*. *Some sumbitch breaks into my house I'll keel 'em*. Or, *He was trespassing' on my property, so I keeled him*. Or some other redneck, stupidly arrogant boast. No, this could cause you grief beyond your dreams, even if you are well within the comfort zone provided by the law.

In Florida, this protection can be very liberal. (See Florida Statute 776, Justifiable Use Of Force, for a complete interpretation) As I read the law and have seen it applied, if you find someone in your home that is not welcome or justified to be there, it is assumed— prima facia evidence—that the intruder intends to commit a felony. That allows you to use deadly force to repel him. This also covers intruders into your car or confrontations on the street. It is a law that doesn't require you to take an ass-whuppin' before you retaliate.

Still, *The Magic Words* that the cops and prosecutors want to hear are like these. Best of all, spoken with great remorse: *I didn't want to hurt him but I was terrified. I was afraid for myself—or my family—and didn't know what else to do. I was so frightened. I was scared to death. I didn't have any choice that I could see*. If you *thought* you saw a weapon in their hand that helps, too. Gun, knife, scissors, something *shiny*. You were so upset it was hard to tell.

Stuff like that. These are *The Magic Words*. Granted, not something John Wayne might say, but essential language to keep you in that comfy home you've just so courageously defended.

I'm not a lawyer but over the years I've have seen several folks put themselves, needlessly, in jail with their mouth. All were men. Women usually admit they were scared to death--as everyone should.

So if it happens to you, call the cops, and your lawyer, remember *The Magic Words* and pat yourself on the back for the good work you've done.

REASONS NOT TO OFF YOURSELF Cops have to learn to deal with sad situations. One of the worst is suicide. Folks who've enjoyed all of this life they can stand. Because of the prevalence of these cases, we all got to know Dr. Jose Lombillo well. Jose was the City's contract psychiatrist at the time and one of the founders of the Mental Health Association in Naples.

Yep, it's a sad business but there can be rewards. Sometimes you can convince those who've tried and failed that there are other options. To seek professional help. Call Jose. Analyze the situation and see that voiding your warranty is not necessary.

I was regularly amazed at the situations a suicide-seeker had determined was so unbearable they could tolerate no more. I'm not talking about physical pain from cancer or terrors like *tic douloureux*--that causes mind-numbing pain, usually incurable. I'm talking about the miseries of the mind, resulting from things the victim has fixated on. Some, very strange.

My dog doesn't love me anymore. What? *The people at work conspire to take all the best parking spaces.* Huh? *I'm in love with Paris Hilton and she doesn't even know I exist.* Paris Hilton? That skink? Bubba, you *are* in need of help.

Seems silly, right. But not to the person with the fixation. To them it's the worst problem in the world. A problem that can only be solved by self-termination.

Then there is the most prevalent, and stupid reason of all. All cops have heard this one too many times: *She, or he, or they, are gonna be sorry when I'm gone.* If you have toyed with the idea of taking a dirt nap to relieve your woes, for Lord's sake this is the worst reason there is. *Be sorry when you're gone!* Bull-pucky! They'll likely be tickled to death you're out of the way.

These scumbags have demonstrated how much they love you by making your life so miserable you want to cash in your frequent cryer miles. And you think they're gonna be sorry when you're gone? Nope. Seen it a thousand times. Your ex-love will be flirting with the cop that delivers the sad news. Forget it.

So, if you've ever been down in the dumps and contemplated how to punish your unrequited lover, leave suicide out. Me, I was always a fan of letting the air outta their tires and throwing away the valve stems. Sugar in the gas tank. Posting their phone number in public restrooms with the message *For anal sex call* . . . Stuff like that.

There, I've just saved your life. Aren't you happy?

THE OLD NAPLES PD

The old Naples PD at 8th and 8th South. The Fire Dept is attached to the right and the Council Chambers are next door on the left. Across the street is Cambier Park.

If you look closely you can see the leg of the old water tower to the left. It was one of Naples' tallest structures at the time. A landmark. It was also a good way for cops to make much needed extra cash.

The tower had a flashing light on top to warn aircraft. The light required maintenance and cops clamored for a chance to make big extra money. That was $15 to climb to the top, replace the bulb, and come back. Who could turn down a fortune like that?

Course, nothin' comes easy. You were required to wear a safety belt and click to it a rider that slid up and down a cable beside the ladder. Supposed to save you if you slipped off the ladder. Trouble was the cable was so rusted, it was like dragging up a hundred extra pounds. So, we disconnected the safety clip and went bare-assed.

Another problem was the ladder tilted backwards when you got to the giant tank on top. That required you hang on the ladder leaning backwards, defying gravity. But, for $15 one expects a few perils.

Jack Bliss had this plum until he was promoted to a level he could get by on his regular salary. Being a good friend, Jack gave the job to me. And I was such a happy, grateful camper.

Strange what you'll do when that ol' wolf is snapping and growling at your door.

Photo courtesy Chester Keene

YOU CAN'T GO THAR   After leaving the NPD, Sandy and I moved to The Great State of Tennessee. After a while, I got back into law enforcement--having found nothing else was so much fun for me. We lived in a town I like to call Bashful Beaver.

Once, while I was on the SO there, I received a call from dispatch asking my 10-20 (location). "Slippery Hollow." I replied.

There was silence for a moment, then the Shift Sergeant interrupted, "SlipperyHoller?"

"10-4."

Next, urgently, "Get outta there and 56 (meet) me at the Church of the Bountiful Backslider Bashers."

I did. The Sergeant was agitated. "Didn't anyone tell you about Slippery Holler?" he said.

"Nope," I answered.

"We don't go down there. Can't go down there."

"Can't go down there? Why the hell not? We're cops, we can go anywhere in our jurisdiction."

"Normally, yeah. But not Slippery Holler."

"What's so special 'bout Slippery Holler?"

"You see that house on the hill at the mouth of the holler?"

"Yep."

"Well, the ol' man that lives in there will shoot down on ya with his long rifle."

"You mean Mr. Walker?" I asked.

"Yeah. . .you know Mr. Walker?"

"Know the whole family," I said. "Coached three of their boys in Pop Warner football."

"That explains it," Sarge said. "They recognized you. Otherwise you'd a been dodgin' bullets."

I was stunned. "I don't understand. These are good people. Why would they shoot at folks."

"It's just the old man. And nobody that ever got close enough to ask, survived," he said.

While my head was still spinning, he went on. "'Nother thing, "There's one other holler we don't go down. On the east end of the county, near the line. Called "Booger Holler."

"Who's shootin' at us up there?"

"Don't know, never caught anyone. But every time a cop car starts down it, some one does. Have a still up there, most likely."

I never did get used to the way law enforcement worked in East Tennessee. Things they did and accepted as normal I could never accommodate. I returned to Florida in six-months.

ON THE SLIPPERY SLOPE   Bashful Beaver caused me to appreciate how different policing in a different state can be. And how much the same.

I've mentioned the different folks and critters and laws to be contended with, but left out one of the most important differences: Geography. Terrain.

Bashful Beaver, in East Tennessee, is mountain and foothill country. Winding roads, steep banks and precipices are ubiquitous. And have to be respected.

Late one Saturday night I came upon skid marks disappearing

over the road's edge and down a steep bank. Investigating, I found a Ford Falcon bellied out in a field fifteen-feet below. The car was fairly smashed up but the driver, protected by the *Angel of the Drunk and Stupid*, bore not a scratch. "How 'bout givin' me a hand up," he said.

The bank was muddy and slick where his car had slid down it. It wasn't going to be any fun but that's why I was making the big bucks. I grabbed a sapling's branch for stability, took a couple of tenuous steps down the bank and held out my hand. My customer, tanked with liquid stupid, could barely walk. But he did have enough coordination to grab my hand in both of his and yank with all his might. I, of course, came skidding down the bank, now muddier and nastier looking than the crash victim. I tried to get back up the bank but it was slicker than Ol' Willie, so try as I might, there I remained.

After seeing the wrecked car, I'd tried to call in dispatch and tell them what I had, but dispatch hadn't answered—probably taking a refreshing nap--and the only other car on duty was out at an all-night burger joint. "May be a long night," I said to my soused companion."

Finally, a good soul saw my empty car, stopped to see what was up, and called the fire department. The car required a wrecker, the drunk and I a long tug rope. I remember I had on a new pair of cowboy boots and it took a month to get all the mud off them.

Another time, I was on a back road at night and saw a Lincoln half off the road, balancing precariously and teetering on the edge over a healthy precipice. I called for help. At the car, I was greeted by a drunk. "Get me the hell outta here," he yelled trying to open the door. With each of his jerky movements, the Lincoln swayed up and down. I jumped on the rear bumper to try to counter-balance the thing, while yelling at the drunk to keep still. He wouldn't and I was sure that any second, car, drunk and I would crash to the bottom.

Finally, help arrived in the form of a wrecker who put his hook around the rear axel and tightened up, stabilizing the Lincoln. I stepped onto the road's welcome, firm surface and said to the drunk, "Now just stay there until we pull the car back."

"I ain't waitin' a damn minute longer," he said, rolling down the window, crawling through, and falling a hundred feet or so through tree limbs, brush, and rocky outcroppings.

When the emergency folks finally got to him he was a scruffed up mess. But not nearly as much as he deserved.

THE COLONEL Bob Burhans, a retired Marine Colonel, was the Undersheriff most of the time I worked for the Collier County Sheriff's Office. The Undersheriff runs the day-to-day operations of the agency, leaving the Sheriff free for his other multiple duties.

Aside from his being a Marine, he was a favorite of mine because of his superb leadership and the fact that on several occasions he "saved my behind." *(It was political matters and The Colonel never mentioned it to me. I didn't even know he had interceeded on my behalf until I retired. That's typical of Bob Burhans)*

Contemporary Marines can tell you many stories about The Colonel. This is a favorite. In 1972, The Colonel was made commander of the 7th Marine Regiment at Camp Pendleton, California. At his inauguration, his address was short and sweet. He said he was pleased to be back and gave his first order to the troops: *Prepare To March.* And the next day at 0600 hrs they did.

The Colonel led them on a 22 mile jaunt, toting everything they had: field gear, records, typewriters, office equipment, you name it. When junior officers complained that the gear could get ruined in the field, Burhans countered that in battle they could face the same situation and now was a good time to make field repairs and learn how to deal with it.

It was a memorable occasion for the 7th Marines. So memorable, that the next commander made Col Bob Burhans'

first order, "Prepare to March," the regiment's motto. It remains so to this day.

Three Chiefs--*G.D. Young, Tom Weschler, Ben Caruthers*

Jack Gant and Curtis Mills examine a rifle siezed as evidence. Jack was the backbone of Fingerprinting and the Training Unit for years. Curtis, spent the majority of his career in CID, where he was

the commander for a number of years.

98

Double-Dippers

Double-dippers Dave Lester (left) and Ken Ferrell (right) worked for both the NPD and the CCSO. The gent in the middle is Dave's brother-in-law--we think.

This was taken after a good day's fishing. One shouldn't look too closely at the contraption used to trap dinner. It may not have been strickly within the bounds of the State of Florida Hunting and Fishing Regulations.

Photo of CCSO from the 60's. Many of these Deputies have passed on. Wish we could identify all of them but we can't. Maybe you'll recognize a few.

Darwin "Bunky" Muir

Bunky was one of the best-liked Cops on the old Naples Police Department. From New Jersey-- not quite *The Shore*--he was a *Situation* long before the dude with the abs showed up.

POLICE DEPARTMENT PERSONNEL - AUGUST, 1964

From left: Policeman 1st Class Winebrenner, Desk Officer Kaester, Sergeant Bliss, Sergeant Bass, Desk Officer Wall, Sergeant Alexander, Policeman 1st Class Spohn, Policeman 1st Class Jones, Policeman 1st Class Hayes, Patrolman Grimm, Patrolman Young, Chief-of-Police Caruthers.
Missing: Desk Officer Holzhausen, Patrolman Dampier.

NPD August 1964

Three Sheriffs

From left, then Chief Deputy Roy Atkins, Sheriff Louis Thorp and later to be Sheriff, Doug Hendry. Doug was know as "Cowboy" in those days for his love of cowboy hats, boots, and a two-gun rig. They are standing in front of the old Evergaldes Courthouse and Jail.

The NPD in the 1070's

Like most cops, multiple jobs were necessary to make ends meet. Once, I drew political cartoons for the Naples Star. They paid me $15 per cartoon and than was good money in the 60's. Also drew cartoons for magazines, but that work wasn't as reliable.

My stint with The Star abrutly ended when one of my cartoons depicted Lyndon Johnson as a Bozo. Accurate, but not flattering. Back then, Collier County was all Democratic and soon I was looking for yet another source of extra income. Above is one of Sam Bass

Daily News art by Don Goodman

Rogers, left, and Young challenge each other.

Sheriff, Police Chief To 'Battle' in Canoes

By JONI RIEDMILLER
Staff Writer

The first annual Jaycees canoe race will feature a jousting match with firefighters and a race between Sheriff Aubrey Rogers and Police Chief Gary Young at 10 a.m. Saturday, Sept. 16, at Central Mall. The race is sponsored by the Central Mall Merchants Association. All proceeds will go to the Naples Boy Scout fund for a trip to Taiwan next summer.

"We expect to have a big turnout for this event," said Ron Gill, publicity chairman for the Jaycees. "The grand prize is a $285 Indian River canoe and merchants at the mall are donating prizes for the samller races." Everyone who enters the race will receive a McDonald's certificate.

THE ENTRY fee for the grand prize race is $20 for each canoe. Entry fee for the other races — the 500, 1,500 and 2,500 springs — is $5 for each canoe for each race. A $25 fee will cover all the races.

Categories for the races are: boys and girls, age 8 to 12; boys and girls, age 13 to 15 and men and women over 16.

Rogers and Young challenged each other to the canoe race; the Jaycees will have a jousting match against the East Naples Fire Department.

County Commissioner Tom Archer has challenged Mayor Roland B. Anderson, or anyone from the city council to a canoe race, Gill said.

"**THE BACK** Bay Marina is providing a barge for the canoe officials to watch the races and we're going to have deputy mobile homes set up to sell hotdogs and soft drinks," Gill said. The Scouts will hold various activities at the mall. Some will be dressed in Taiwan Scout uniforms.

Contestants will be able to park their cars and launch their canoes in the parking lots of Pancake Palace and Benson Insurance agency.

Canoe rentals are available for $5. Anyone wishing further information may call 261-3558 or 774-2164.

THE FIRST CANOE RACE

Hee-Haw Alive and Well

My wife Sandy and I at a charity event for the JayCees. We sang "Where, Where, Are You Tonight," from the Hee-Haw TV show with lyrics appropriate for Naples.

The crowd at the Naples Yacht Club was delighted--- when we were finished.

Long Time No Come See

My retirement causes me to smile like a jackass eating briars because I know I'm going home and won't be at the Sheriff's Office any longer. Sheriff Hunter is smiling for the same reason

Choir Practice
Session Seven

TIMEX VS THE SIPPY HOLE John Cameron Swayze said it, and said it, and said it: "Takes a lickin' and keeps on tickin'." The Timex watch tagline was one of the most repeated in its day. On one of those days Timex was in Naples.

A series of commercials pitted the durable Timex against abuse far above normal. Shown tied to boat bottoms, run over by cars, trampled by horses, after the action was over the camera would zoom in on the watch and show the rugged time piece still running. *Takes a lickin' and keeps on tickin'*. And it was all true. Kinda.

When Timex came to Naples they chose the Swamp Buggy track's Sippy Hole as a suitable challenge for the ticker. Sheriff Doug Hendry was filmed, for the commercial, driving a swamp buggy, with a Timex taped to one of the huge airplane tires. When the buggy exits, the camera switches to the watch that "keeps of ticking."

The part they left out was Doug went back to work after a couple of runs and left Deputy Don Harris--then with the CCSO and later a city cop with the NPD--to drive the buggy the rest of the day.

Don did it. And did it. And did it. All day long until the director finally got the shot he was looking for--a Timex that was still running after the thumping and dunking.

The commercials, you see, were legit. *They just didn't tell you how many times it took to get one to survive the beating.*

Don was sent residuals--payments for every time the commercial was aired--for several years thereafter. He donated them to the Junior Deputy program.

Don't know what happened to all the watches that drowned in the Sippy Hole.

MORE DUNKIN' To sell products, more than Timex watches got dunked in the Swamp Buggy track's Sippy Hole. A soap or skin lotion commercial--I forget which--took turns driving two lovely

106

girls through the goop. Again, they did it all day long.

The girls would get all made up, hair coiffed, and dressed in clean shirts and jeans, then mount a woods buggy and be driven through ol' Sippy, coming out soggy and muddy as a ground hog. Then, they'd spruce them up again, and film how wonderful their skin looked after using the soap or whatever they were selling. And they did look wonderful. Never seen such beautiful skin on a human. I told one of the girls so.

She said, "I hope so, that's why they hire me. I'm a *skin* model."

I must have looked confused.

"I was blessed with skin that has no blemishes," she said. "No freckles, birthmarks, nothing. Thank god, it's very rare and allows a few of us to make a nice living showing how *all women* can look if they use the product we're advertising at the time. Course it's a lie, but it pays well."

She went on. "There are other models with *perfect* parts, too. Hand models, hair, eyes, teeth, you name it."

So I learned another trick of the advertising trade that day and answered a persistent question that had bothered me. *Why there weren't any really decent toilet paper commercials.*

INDUCED LABOR All guns are dangerous, especially *"unloaded"* ones. Of those, unloaded semi-autos top the list. Sometimes a round will hide inside and not be detected by even the most experienced gun handler. Chester Keene remembered that such was the case one evening, long ago, at the NPD.

A Detective, after making a concealed weapons arrest, was checking the gun into evidence with the Evidence Sgt. and Armorer, JD Spohn. Both were experienced with guns, being ex-military and veteran cops.

At the old PD on 8th and 8th South, the evidence closet was in the radio dispatch room. It was a regular closet that besides evidence contained uniforms, a few special weapons, cleaning supplies, and most anything else that needed to be put out of the way. This was not quite the high-security evidence fortresses of today.

The Detective and JD had diligently removed the magazine, and worked the slide several times to eject any bullet that might be in the breach. Nothing. Then the slide was sent home and *BOOM* the gun fired a live round. The round hit the glass dispatcher's desk top, skidded off, and lodged in the wall beside the Dispatcher, Betty Jo Rankin, missing her by inches.

Betty Jo was nine months pregnant and was due to have induced labor the next morning. But, having a bullet zing by your head has a way of getting your attention. And getting your adrenaline pumping like a broken BP well . Such was the case with Betty Jo who, later that evening, gave birth to a healthy baby boy--induced by a .38.

BE CAREFUL WHAT YOU PRAY FOR Chester Keene was a bailiff in the Collier County Criminal Court on the morning this tale took place. As he tells it:

I was working as Lead Bailiff and a Deputy we'll call Thumper Hopkins was the Assistant Bailiff. Thumper was controlling the door to the holding cell in the next room where the inmates waited for their appearance before the judge. Thumper wasn't wearing a firearm, as was a rule of the court, and for protection carried a 30,000 volt "stun" baton, a *polite* name for a *cattle prod*. Thumper also did the fingerprinting, when required, so he was in close contact with the inmates in court and needed some protection.

Suddenly, there arose a commotion coming from the holding cell that was so loud it was disruptive to the court proceedings. An inmate was giving a fire and brimstone sermon that Cryin' Jimmy would have been proud of, screaming with all the lung power he could muster: "*The Lord will take his vengeance on those in this courtroom by striking them down with a bolt of lightning. Take my word, sinners.*"

The overwhelming uproar continued until the judge demanded that the inmate be brought before him, forthwith.

Thumper disappeared through the connecting door, there was bloodcurdling howl, then silence and Thumper reappeared in the doorway.

"What happened?" the judge asked.

"He got that bolt of lightnin' he was prayin' for." Thumper said, holding up his electric cattle prod.

SWAMP BUGGY DAZE Part One During the first week I lived

in Naples, I got involved with Swamp Buggy Days. It was 1956 and, having taken the five minutes necessary to see the town, I was wondering just why my Dad had decided to move here. There was nothing. Maybe a couple thousand folks, tops. Two traffic lights.

When evening came, I moved with dejection to the solace of an ungentlemanly bar on the East Trail called *The 41 Club*. I was nursing a beer I'd never seen before or since. It was called *Old Dutch Ale* and the bottle seemed to be made of clay.

I was wondering if I should risk gaging down another when the Hank Williams on the juke box was overwhelmed by the entrance of three bearded, rowdy men. They proceeded to question each bar patron, soon coming to me. "Where's your badge?" One asked me.

"Don't have one," I said, wondering why he though I was a cop.

"Don't mean that kind. Your *Swamp Buggy Badge.*"

I just looked at him, having no idea what a Swamp Buggy Badge was.

"You don't have a beard, so you have to have a badge," he explained. "If not, you're gonna have to go to jail."

What the hell was going on.

"Okay, then," my interrogator said, taking me by the arm, "let's go to jail."

Before I knew what was happening, I was taken outside and placed in an all-bar jail cell on wheels, being towed by a pickup truck. There were three others in there with me, all drinking beers from a case on the floor, and having, a grand time.

When we got underway, one of the other *prisoners* explained what *was* going on. During the weeks before Swamp Buggy Race Day, all adult men were required to either grow a beard or pay one dollar for a Swamp Buggy badge sold by the JayCees. It was a popular Naples tradition, the money going to charity.

After I realized what was going on and relaxed, it turned out be a great evening. We bounced along to every bar in town, collecting badge-less and beardless errants, all the while being supplied with an endless supply of beer. When the bars closed at two, we were released, by now as rowdy as our jailers and drunker than Hogan's Goat. It was an introduction to Naples I'll never forget.

Somewhere over the years, the tradition has died. No beards. No badges. Since the Bush Patrol gents put you in the jail using whatever force was necessary, I suspect some sleazy lawyer sued and ruined it.

We're the less for it.

SWAMP BUGGY DAZE Part Two Each year another Swamp Buggy Days tradition took place. The mobile jail cell, used to raise money for charity each year, was owned by the Naples JayCees. Somewhere along the line it became tradition for local high school students to steal the jail. And place it in the damnedest places.

No matter how inventive the JayCees were in hiding the jail, the students were just as sly in finding it. And where they moved the jail to caused some of us to wonder how they pulled it off. I suspect collusion on the part of some of the NPD cops. How else could you drag a jail cell on a trailer around town in the middle of the night and not be seen?

Where did it appear? Once the missing jail was found at the end of the pier. Several times in local parks. Another time in front of the NPD headquarters building. And Dave Dampier remembers perhaps the most baffling; on the roof of the Sunshine Hardware on 5th Ave South.

How'd they do that? Damned if I know but it was always fun trying to figure it out.

SWAMP BUGGY DAZE Part Three The Swamp Buggy Parade meant a ton of extra work for the NPD each year. Most cops, however, loved the event as it guaranteed the kind of off-the-wall action and dark humor cops thrive on.

The parade itself was unique. Starting at 3rd Street South and 12th Avenue, it turned the corner at 5th Ave, marched up the main business drag to 8th St So and disbanded in Cambier Park. Aside from the bands, commercial floats, politicians, and array of traditional wood's buggies and racing buggies seen nowhere else, there were other unique participants.

Some found it strange that the mobile units that drew the most cheers were the City Of Naples garbage trucks. The crowd lining the street, roared their approval. And, it seemed genuine, not mock, furor.

In any parade mistakes occur. The Swamp Buggy had their share. On one float, there was a miniature shrimp boat with a smoke stack that puffed white smoke. Somewhere along the parade route, some rascal slipped a condom over the stack, and as the parade proceeded the thing grew to gigantic proportions, delighting the crowd.

Then there were the "arrests" made out of the crowd by the Bush Patrol posse attending the Swamp Buggy jail. Some folks didn't see the humor in being rousted from the crowd and protested with vigor. There were times, when the arrests turned into near bar-fight bedlam. (We tried not to "see" these things)

There were also lessons to be learned. Each year, one of the floats had a "swamp creature" who'd roll off the float and *terrorize* watchers. The critter was actually a man, covered with Spanish Moss until he looked like a dangerous clump of weeds. Occasionally, about halfway through the parade, the critter would begin an impassioned dance, ripping off the Spanish Moss and his clothing. Crackers knew the problem and roared with laughter.

Using Spanish Moss for a body decoration is fine if you first boil the stuff. This kills the chiggers that infest the moss and soon, if not killed, will burrow deep in the wearer's hide.

Yep, there were lessons to be learned, especially if you want to insure all those majorettes and parade marchers don't slip an' slide along the route. That lesson? All the horses in a parade go last.

SWAMP BUGGY DAZE **Part Four** Nowadays, some of the best swamp buggy drivers are women. Men and women race equally. There was a time women could only run in a special race called *The Powder Puff.* And compete for the highly coveted title of *Mud Duchess.*

The majority of these races were won by Liz Chesser, wife of Leonard, or Bonnie Hancock, wife of Lee. Both of these gents are legends in the grimy sport.

Most of the other women in the race had no experience, making the event exciting and unpredictable. My wife Sandy, was one of those who succumbed to the madness. With her passenger, Charlene Graham, she piloted one of Lee Hancock's buggies, the six-cylinder version. They are pictured in the thick of the action. In those days, the track was not as smooth as it is today. There were boulders, logs, and God knows what else hidden under the soupy mud. Driving a high-powered buggy, at speed, through this obstacle course caused many a causality. Broken off wheels were common. Flipped buggies not unusual. Crashes commonplace.

Sandy and Charlene made a good start, plowed through the Sippy Hole, hit a boulder, bounced high is the air, and landed on a steep bank, where they perched, half tipped over. The crowd oohed and aahed when, with each of their movements, the buggy teetered and seemed ready to tip over, dumping them in the water with the huge beast on top of them.

Sitting there, afraid to move, waiting for rescue, there was conversation.

Charlene: "Hope this doesn't tip over, I can't swim."

Sandy: "If it tips over and lands on us, swimming isn't going to be an option. Besides, I can't get out anyway."

The reason Sandy couldn't get out was that being diminutive her legs wouldn't reach the gas pedal. We solved that by duct taping a 2"x4" block on the pedal then taping Sandy's foot to both of them.

I know, I know, it was a stupid thing to do. But with all the excitement, and the mud, and the beer, it seemed like *a real good idea at the time.*

SUPER FUZZ The most unusual vehicle to ever wear the NPD silver badge had to be Super Fuzz. It was a racing buggy that for some reason I had to have. It had a blue light and siren and a terrible paint job.

This was one of the old style racing buggies, before they got sleek and really fast. Later, we built one of the faster variety which allowed me to drive it off the track and into the fence a lot quicker.

Pictured is yours truly at the wheel exiting the Sippy Hole after yet another second place finish. We had all second place finishes, which doesn't sound too bad unless you know there were only two buggies in a heat race.

Riding behind me is Bill Beatty. At the time buggies all carried a co-pilot. In my case he was necessary because the shifter for the automatic transmission was where he sat. He did the shifting. I know, don't ask.

Bill survived my wild driving and is now the Chief of Police in Wauchula, Florida.

We finally built, with the help of Domestic Welding, a beautiful buggy powered with a 650hp Dodge Magnum engine. And some of the most valuable help came from Lee Hancock, Leonard Chesser, and Lonnie Chesser. These guys, who were supposed to be the competition lent their experience--unselfishly--to help get the job done. They were always that way. In one race, when I flattened a tire, Leonard took one off on one of his buggies for me to use.

The new buggy was fast, powerful, and capable of winning. Trouble was, I was much better at wrecking buggies than driving them. On my last run, I hydroplaned and took out about 20 feet of chain-link fence.

Drawing is of the logo the author drew for Swamp Buggy, Inc. in the 70's. It was the official logo for years, until the new style of buggies made the drawing out of date.

BOSS TRUSTEE Some accepted procedures in jails a few years ago would, today, land Sheriffs and Chiefs in their own jail. Today, we've oversteered in the other direction: too many rights. But, you can see where it came from.

A good friend of mine got in the law enforcement business because of his size, considerable strength, and ability to open up a barrel of whup-ass. He was hired at the Immokalee Road Camp when it was privately operated by contract with the County. Being physically in control of the prisoners was very important in those days. Still is, but jailers aren't allowed to do it.

Another revered concept was the "Boss Trustee" or "Head Smasher" or other sobriquet that appropriately indicated a convict who was *large and in charge*. The boss trustee freed jailers of the tiring and sometimes messy job of beating unruly prisoners.

It worked like this. Lets say there was a prisoner, usually some punk that didn't know how to make time, who was a disquieting factor in the lockdown. The Boss Trustee would get the keys, lock himself in the cell with the Ahole and take care of business. You seldom had any more trouble with a jerk after the Boss Trustee had tuned him up.

Sometimes, a prisoner was causing trouble in more subtle ways that the Boss Trustee hadn't noticed. Then, you'd give him the word: "You have a turd back there in cell 2 that's crapping in your sand box." This simple alert always produced the desired corrective action, with the troublemaker soon a bruised but compliant camper in the Crossbar Motel.

Experienced prisoners, especially ex-cons who'd done a lotta time, knew how to *make time* and seldom disrupted tranquility. Most would sleep about 20 hours a day.

But the young, self-proclaimed badasses were sometimes a bother. Until they met the Boss Trustee.

Ah, for the good 'ol days.

BANK SECURITY NAPLES STYLE Was a time banks, to keep their FDIC Insurance valid, had to have a security check by the local cops. At least, the two banks here, Bank of Naples and First National, did. We alway found so many security mistakes we called the inspections "*Insecurity, keep your money under the mattress*" checks. This lax mentality was understandable since neither institution had ever been robbed, at least in recent memory. So the bank's mind set was: *Why bother, who's gonna rob a bank in The Elephant's Graveyard?*

Actually, the First National Bank didn't do a *terrible* job with security. It was Miz Mamie Tooke's Bank of Naples that needed the tune-up.

As an example, they'd just installed drive-up windows in the alley behind the bank--four or five of them. The FDIC required that money delivered to an exterior drive-up booth be supplied through some method that keeps the cash secure. Pneumatic tubes, something like that, connecting to the main building. Mamie's bank didn't do that. Don't know how she got around the rule but she *wouldn't* do it. Too expensive. Each booth was self contained and free standing. To get the money out there in the morning, a clerk wheeled a cart with $45,000 for each window on it. Just a clerk, no guard, or nuttin'.

I talked to Miz Tooke about this *just-asking-for-it* practice. She said she'd start having a guard go with them, but she never did.

Another problem was the clerks sat in those little remote booths all day *with all that money.* Sitting duckies for a robber.

Mamie wasn't worried about this either. The booths were bulletproof, she said. And the rear entrance door was steel with good locks. I told her they were still vulnerable and if I wanted to rob them how I'd do it.

I went to a booth and knocked on the rear door. "Who is it?" came the response.

I mumbled an unintelligible name.

In a second the door was unlocked and opened and a clerk, surprised to see me and Miz Tooke said, "Who. . .?"

All the clerks in the other booths fell for the same scam when I knocked. So much for locks.

Mamie was aghast and said she'd take care of that. But I don't think she ever did.

I believe that Mamie was so cavalier about security because she knew that no one that knew her--and that was everyone in Naples-- was fool enough to rob her and evoke her considerable rage.

And she was probably right cause it never happened.

MORE TALES OF MIZ TOOKE The Bank of Naples had another practice that was totally insane. At the close of business each day, tens-of-thousands of dollars were loaded in the back of one of the employee's personal sedan, and she drove it to the Federal Reserve Bank in Ft. Myers so it could be securely locked up. Not quite a Wells Fargo armored car and easy pickin's for a robber. Of course it never happened.

The employee, a petite redhead named Barbara, realizing the danger, wasn't real thrilled about this assignment but, valuing her job, didn't think it was wise to go against Miz Tooke's wishes.

When my wife, Sandy, worked for a S&L in Bonita, they did the same thing, taking the proceeds in a private car each day to a local bank.

But, if you wanted a good old fashioned bank that really cared for their customers, Miz Tooke's Bank of Naples was your first stop. Dave Dampier remembers:

When I was in my preteens my Dad, a commercial net fisherman of sometimes uncertain means, would need some cash for "tide-over" money until the next run. He would walk into the Bank of Naples front door, make a slight right turn and be in front of Miz Mamie's desk. At the time it sat in the front lobby near the door.

She'd quickly greet him: "Hello Clyde". He'd say something like "Miz Mamie I need two or three hundred dollars". She would reach in a drawer and withdraw a "90 Day Note" form and ask the amount he *really* needed, he'd tell her and she'd pen in the amount then direct him to "Sign here". In five minutes he'd be on his way with the cash.

Sandy and I also used this handy service. One call and the money was waiting when we got there. Last time I used it was for a very important expense: to buy a stock car.

THE HOOT OWL SHIFT Cops around here traditionally call the all-night 11 to 7 shift "The Hoot Owl Shift." Chester Keene remembers this tale from these dark and mysterious hours.

A Patrolman was reporting how the windshield on his patrol car had been broken. He prefaced it by saying, "I know you're not going to believe this, Sarge, but this is exactly what happened." He had good reason to add this caveat.

Said the Patrolman: While on routine patrol, on Mooringline Drive at approximately 0300 hours, I received a call reference a prowler in the area. It was raining (drizzle) and due to the amount of street light I turned off my headlights so they wouldn't alert the prowler to my presence. I left the windshield wipers on so I could see the road, houses, etc.

All of a sudden, out of nowhere, this owl swooped down and attacked my wiper blade. It must have looked some kind of prey to him. His feet (talons) got caught between the blade and the glass. I turned my wipers on fast speed but could not get him off.

I got out of my car with my Maglite. The bird was flapping his wings, going back and forth with each beat of the wipers. I, not thinking, swung at the owl with my metal flashlight, trying to

117

dislodge him. In doing so I broke the windshield.

The owl, now fearing for his life, his eyes as big as two softballs, pried himself free and escaped into the night. End of report.

Chester said: I considered the report, wondering how anyone--not just me but those up the chain of command who would read it-- could believe this wild yarn. But, the only advice I could offer the Patrolman was, "Couldn't you just say a coconut fell on it?"

YOUR TAX DOLLARS AT WORK There was a friend of the family, the age of my oldest son, Wayde, who was as likable a young man as you'd ever hope to meet. Buddy, we'll call him, had a ready smile, was polite with a good sense of humor. I always enjoyed seeing him in our home when he came by to visit.

Problem was, he got involved with some Aholes that led him into the narcotics business, where he got arrested on a federal smuggling charge and sent to prison--straight to prison, do not pass Go.

Buddy did his time without incident and we didn't see him again for a few years. Then, one day, I ran into him on the street. After a warm greeting--I still liked the guy and still do--I asked him what he'd been doing. "Captaining a yacht for a rich dude," he said.

"Well," I said, joking, "I guess you were experienced in that line from the smuggling business."

Buddy laughed. "Yeah, but that was a whole different thing," he said. "I didn't have a Captain's license, then."

"So how'd you get it?" I asked.

"When I was released from prison, as part of my parole, I had to complete some occupational classes--learn a trade. At the government's expense. And they, seeing I'd been a smuggler, decided I should get a Captain's license so, in case I went back into the business, I could do it right." He laughed. "Just kidding about the last. But I did wonder why they were training a smuggler to be better at his job."

I was, too, considering the number of ex-cons that go right back into crime. How stupid could you get? What was next? *Accounting for Embezzlers? Graphic Arts for Forgers? Auto Mechanics for Car Thieves?*

But, I was wrong. Buddy never returned to crime and still has a dream job as a Captain on a wealthy man's yacht. And has been doing it for many years.

And he's still as likable as ever.

THEY DON'T????? Russ Davis, an old friend and former Deputy at the CCSO, remembered this story from years ago. He'd received a call from Lynn Bailey and she was laughing so hard she could barely speak. Lynn was a fixture in Old Naples, hostess of a popular daily show on *WNOG* radio, and wife of a prominent doctor. She was involved with every charity going and had such a warm personality it made your day just to talk to her. And it certainly made Russ' that day.

Lynn was on her way to work, she said, driving her sporty little car the way she always drove it: fast. Her driving would get your attention and she soon drew that of a Florida Highway Patrolman. (Russ said the name of the officer has been lost to history. Or at least the two prime suspects, still around, won't make any admissions.)

Lynn pulled over and the Trooper came up to the window. Without waiting for the Trooper to speak, she said, "I'll bet I know why you stopped me."

The Trooper, surprised by her candor said, "What would that be?"

"You want me to buy tickets to *The Policeman's Ball*." (A popular annual event put on by the NPD)

"Ma'mm," the cop said, indignantly, "FHP Troopers *don't have balls!*"

Ooops.

Haven't seen Lynn for a while. Russ, when he told us the story, was still laughing.

DURWOOD One of the calls I always dreaded getting was one that had *"Durwood"* in the message. It usually mean that Durwood was drunk and fighting in one of the bars. And Durwood, a big, strong, block-layer, was an all-day-sucker when it came to fighting. The irony was when sober he was a soft-spoken guy you'd never expect could punch you in the head and make it ring like the cathedral bells at St. Patrick's on Christmas Eve.

Once, when he was sober, I inquired as to why he turned into *Mr. Hyde* when tanked on liquid stupid. He said, "I just can't stand someone putting their hands on me when I'm drunk. Or giving me orders, bossing me around. If you have to arrest me again, just tell me *'Durwood, you have to leave'* and I'll go with you. Long as you don't lay hands on me."

I engraved that advice in bold letters in my *Golden Book On Staying Alive*. And it wan't long before I got to use it. The call was like this: "Durwood is over at the Anchor. He's done throwed one guy through the back-bar mirror and's workin' on two more." Unfortunately, I was just two-blocks away and couldn't hide.

When I arrived, Durwood was taking a breather, chugging a beer, while several other combatants, their shirts ripped and heads lumped, staggered for the door. I tried out the magic words.

"Durwood," I said, with due respect, "it's time to go."

Durwood looked at me and said, "Okay if I finish my beer first?"

"Certainly," I said with a sigh of relief. Hell, he coulda had two long as I didn't have to rassle him.

We were just exiting the side door, I behind Durwood, when things turned bad. He couldn've added to the advice he gave me about coming peacefully, *"This don't apply to Jack Bliss."* He and Jack hated each other. Anyway, guess who was just outside the door, having hurried to the scene, alway eager for a brawl: Jack Bliss. "Get your ass in that police car," he said, grabbing him.

Durwood roared, and cocked his right. I locked my arms around his chest from behind. He stomped down on my toes, making my foot hurt so badly it still throbs when I drive by the Anchor's old site on US 41. And the fight was on.

We finally got him out to the palm tree beside the street and, so we could take a breather, handcuffed his arms around it. He began to charge around it like *Little Black Sambo*, until finally, and mercifully for us, he collapsed and we were able to haul him down to the City Jail. Normally, serenity would've returned to The Elephant's Graveyard. Not so, tonight.

It wasn't an hour until a frantic call went out, "Durwood's back at the Anchor." When I got there--thank The Almighty--he'd already gone home after inflicting only minor damage to property and customers.

Turns out, we had a Sergeant on duty who was in a religious phase and thought that all living things were noble and of some worth. *Right.* He'd turned Durwood loose. Later, when I asked him why he said, "Oh, I talked with him, prayed over him and I was assured he'd seen the error of his ways."

My only comment was, "Next time he gets drunk and tears up the Anchor and half its customers, *you* go get him. And you'd better bring Jesus with ya."

WHAT KEPT ME HONEST In the 50's and 60's Georgia was so notorious for the bogus traffic tickets given to Yankees that the AAA routed drivers around the entire state. If you drove through Georgia in a car with a New York, New Jersey, or other northern plate you were going to get a ticket. How? Small cities had a bad habit of abruptly lowering the speed limit, or hiding traffic lights in trees, or stop signs behind bushes. Once, in Georgia, a CCSO Deputy was put in the same cell as the prisoner he was extraditing. The Deputy's crime: running a hidden stop sign. Cost Sheriff Doug Hendry $100 to get him out.

It got so shameful that a Georgia state law enforcement agency finally stepped in. Disguising agents as tourists, they'd wait until the sleazy traffic net was dropped on them, then spring their own trap, arresting the thieves in uniforms.

That's when I discovered that cops, in *sting* operations, *would arrest cops.* It was one of the things that kept me honest on the job for over 40 years.

Then there was the thing about taking bribes. One of my mentors, Chief Ben Caruthers, explained it to me early on. "Before you take that bribe," he said, "do some mathematics. Figure out how much money you'll probably make over your law enforcement career. Then how much in retirement you're likely to collect. Then calculate how much a lawyer is going to cost you if you get caught. Add it all up and if the bribe isn't more than that--what you'll be losing when you're in jail and out of law enforcement--it's not a smart financial move."

Next, you have to worry about the jail thing. Cops in jail usually have to be put in protective custody to stay alive. You're in a jungle where cop *killers* are revered as heros. The only thing in prison more hated is a child molester. Made me wonder, recently, when I saw a local cop was accused of being a child molester and another with kiddie porn on his computer. If these guys are found guilty and sent to the joint. . .

So my motto was *I'm not saying I can't be had, but your offer better be way the hell up there. Enough to replace the lifetime of earnings I'll lose when I get caught.*

Or maybe even my life.

The Carl Strickland Story

Ben Caruthers and I were invited, by Chief Weschler, over to the NPD to participate in a ceremony honoring the PD's fallen officer, Lou Collins. Talking about the event later, Ben told me that Lou wasn't the only officer killed in the line of duty at the NPD. He said the first was Carl Strickland in 1954 and it was so long ago that nobody remembered. We thought that was a damn shame, so I wrote this entry in my blog, Naples 5-Oh.

THE NPD'S FIRST CASUALTY In the early fifties the Naples Police Department suffered its first killed-in-the-line-of-duty officer. His name was Carl Strickland and he worked evenings--or whenever needed--in McDonald's Quarters. He lived there. He was black.

But don't look for Carl in the rolls of deceased warriors. Or on the handsome memorial monument gracing the grounds of NPD's Headquarters. It's not there. Why?

Not because the NPD didn't make a diligent effort to establish the facts in the incident. They did, but after an exhaustive search of the records they were unable to establish to a certainty that Carl was murdered, Or even worked there.

Contemporaries remember Carl well. One, Chief Ben Caruthers, knew Carl, knew his wife, knew he was a NPD officer that worked exclusively in McDonald's Quarters, and that he was murdered in an ambush about two weeks before Caruthers joined the department in 1954. He also remembered that Carl's widow was given a small pension.

Otherwise, the facts are slim and the records long gone--if they ever existed. This is depriving the NPD of one of it's heros and the recognition that Officer Strickland deserves. Let's set the record and history straight.

The Miami News - Nov 8, 1954

Cop's Slayer Sought In State

Special to The Miami Daily News

Naples, Nov. 8 — A statewide alarm was out today for John Wesley, 52, Naples Negro who is sought for the fatal shooting of Naples' first Negro policeman.

The policeman, Carl Strickland, about 45, had been on duty for less than two months.

Naples police said Strickland was shot in the head twice Saturday night, minutes after he broke up a fist fight in the Negro district. They said Wesley, who was seen running from the scene of the shooting, was a party to the fight.

After combing the city of Naples Saturday night and Sunday, Sheriff Roy O. Atkins of Collier County and Cale Jones, Naples police chief, issued an all-points bulletin for Wesley's arrest.

CARL STRICKLAND VERIFICATION Ms Lila Zuck, President of the *Collier County Historical Research Center*, had two pieces of information verifying that Carl Strickland was an NPD cop and that he was murdered. Lila, herself, is a writer having authored the popular *Naples Oldest Tradition, Swamp Buggy Racing.*

This is the first verification, a clipping from the *Miami Daily News.*

Second, is the book *We Also Came* a black history of Collier County by Maria Stone. On page 115 is this quote by John Salter, long-time Naples resident:

"I was the second black policeman here. That was in 1957. The first one, which was before me, was Paul Strickland. He got killed.

We didn't wear uniforms on the police force but we did have a badge, a pistol, and a blackjack. We were policemen assigned to the area where we lived. At that time I lived in McDonald's Quarters. Our authority was in that little neighborhood right there.

I quit after a year. The City paid me, but I already had a regular job working for Benny Morris."

Don't know where the "Paul" came from but it is obviously Officer Strickland.

Further perusal of the book by my wife, Sandy, revealed that on page 33, in an interview with Eddie Sanders, who came here in

1929, he said:

"I can tell you that the first black policemen in Naples were Carl Strickland and Johnny Salters."

That should pretty much put this issue to bed. Let's give this Officer the recognition he deserves.

And thank you, Lila

The Final Word

I am writing this in May of 2011. This month Carl was honored with his name being placed on the wall of honor in Tallahassee and, this week, on the national monument to fallen officers in Washington DC. Credit must be given to the Project Carl's most valuable asset, NPD Office Bill Gonsalves. Bill is the kind of Cop you wouldn't want after you if you were a crook. He doesn't give up.

And to that end, Welcome Home Carl

SUPREME COURT INSANITY The endless questioning of Supreme Court nominee Elena Kagan caused me to think of some local Judges and appraise their work in the office. There are many *good* ones, but three came to mind for their excellence: Judges Hugh Hayes, Dan Monaco, and Harold Smith. I've known these Judges well and they're who I'd want to decide my fate if I was ever called to accountability. And there were times when I could've been.

Why? There's an old maxim in the legal business: *"If you're innocent, ask for a Judge to decide your case. If you're guilty, ask for a jury trial."* A good Judge will see the truth. Juries can be manipulated clowns in a judicial circus.

Now Ms Kagan is participating in another circus, the obligatory hearings to determine if she is fit to sit on the nation's highest bench. And most of the questions are politically motivated, not geared to determine her suitability. It shouldn't make any difference if she's pro or con abortion, or guns, or homosexuality, or RC and Moon Pies. It should only be important that she is *fair* and decides constitutional issues in an unbiased manner.

Still, it's hard to predict. Earl Warren, California's most savage prosecuting attorney, became a Weepy Wet Willie Liberal after he accepted his lifelong, no-control position on the Court.

We must, however, *try* to predict fairness and the only way to do that is to look at the nominee's rulings record as a Judge.

Whadda you mean she's never even been a judge. . . ? The only choice worse than that would be an egghead academic from Harvard.

Choir Practice
Session Eight

GOOD OL' BUBBY Bub was a sweet guy. Those who knew him wondered how he maintained that attitude after working all those years in the Collier County Jail--the jail not being *Fun City*. But Bub always had a sunny disposition, was eager to help, and could take a joke. And that was a good thing because Bub was one of those poor folks who seem to always wear a "Kick Me" sign.

We all screw up and do mindless things. Bub, however, was a repeat offender. He'd do the same ones over and over, never seeming to learn from the experience.

As an example, one of the Jailers would ask Bub if he'd go get them a Coke. Bub, of course, would cause that's the kinda guy he was. The jail has long hallways and you could see Bub heading for the Coke machine for maybe 50 yards. Halfway there, another Jailer would yell to Bub, "Get me one, too." Bub would nod and continue on.

He'd soon return with one Coke, then go back to get the second one. That's right. And he fell for this gag over and over.

Then there was the coffee thing. Bub wore his watch on his left wrist and held his coffee cup in his left hand. When asked what time it was, he'd look at his watch, tipping over the cup and spilling coffee in his lap. Did it time after time.

Bub once called a Kentucky hospital, to determine the condition of a very sick relative. The front office checked, and came back on the line, "I'm sorry, but he's gone."

Bub loaded up his family and headed for KY. There, he went directly to the funeral home, where he was told the relative was not there. Confused, he went to see the hospital folks who told him that they meant the relative had "gone" home. He was fine.

That was Bub.

NITPICK MUNYGRUBBER "Nitpick"--other cops had worse

names for him--was a local attorney. I'm sure he did something worthwhile in his practice but I must've overlooked it. Nitpick was one of the Awipes who sued me. There were others. At one time they amounted to 22 million dollars worth and that was a lotta money in the 70's. I never was much concerned though, cause I knew they were just a few personal injury attorneys and other lowlifes trying to generate an illegitimate buck.

It still happens. If you watch daytime TV almost every ad is some attorney trying to get you to sue someone. Doctors. Auto insurance companies. Or collect Social Security benefits SS says you're not due. And some folks wonder why the cost of health care and auto insurance is what it is. Howsumever, I digress.

Nitpick had found some form, that the City issued to the public, that had an error on it. It caused no one any problem except Nitpick who sued the Mayor, the City Manager, and yours truly--who didn't print the thing, just had his officers hand it out. We all ended up in Federal Court in Miami.

After Nitpick had presented his case, the Judge called the attorneys up to the bench. And in language loud enough for anyone in the courtroom to hear, berated Nitpick in the following manner-or words to this effect:

"After hearing your case, I find it to be the most useless waste of this court's time I've ever encountered. And if you ever bring forth a similar proceeding to me, God help you. You are, however, technically correct and I must give you a directed verdict."

Nitpick, though chastened, was ecstatic. Money!

Then the judge spoke to the jury. "The law requires me to find in the favor of the plaintiff and you are required to award him financial damages. I can advise, you, however that if you award him just *one dollar* this case will be complete and he is finished.

The jury was out a half hour and returned with a *one dollar* award. We each paid 33 1/3 cents.

Come to think of it, that was more than the rest of the frivolous suits collected.

HANDWRITING EVIDENCE There've been some scandals in the news of late about bad evidence causing folks to be wrongfully convicted of crimes. Texas. North Carolina. Even stuff from the FBI lab. Thankfully, DNA evidence is becoming a dominate factor and has rescued many a poor soul who has been wrongfully convicted on eyewitness testibaloney and other less reliable forms of proof.

I was always worried about handwriting analysis. I'm not talking about the sleazy scam of reading character traits by looking at a sample of your writing. *Oh yes, the pressure here and the loops there show that you are a handsome, intelligent, soon-to-be-rich male with a latent love of didgeridoo tunes and a subliminal compulsion to wear Victoria's Secret lingerie.*

Nope, we're talking about the *scientific* comparison of two exemplars to determine if the same person wrote both. What bothers me is I prefer my *scientific* evidence to be over-overwhelmingly certain. Like, "the chances of someone else having this DNA are one in two-hundred-billion." Or, "there is *no other* human with this same fingerprint."

Handwriting experts testify with a lotta "appears", and "looks like", indecisive stuff like that. First one I ever used made me suspicious.

We were prosecuting a forgery case that went to trial. An expert from the FBI lab was our forensic witnesses. I met him before trial and asked about his testimony. He shrugged, sorta noncommittal, and asked, "What kind of case do you have against him."

I told him what we had and that it was strong. He brightened, "Well then, I think we can put this joker away." And on the stand, he did just that causing me to wonder just how he would've testified if I'd said we had a weak case.

Probably just me, but I want that one in two-hundred-billion certainty. At least I would if I was innocent and on trial and there wasn't any DNA or fingerprints to save my bacon. Especially in Texas and North Carolina.

BUDGET SMOKE AND MIRRORS Nowadays, with money being so tight, budget time for government agencies calls for creative planning and innovative ideas. Back in the 70's, at the NPD we had some innovative ideas, too. Just to make things easier and not pee anyone off. Although the procedure was never spoken of, it was a workable constant, that every department head knew. At least we did at the PD. It worked like this.

The City Council would get word to the City Manager how much--what percentage--they were willing to raise the budget for the upcoming year. For the sake of easy math, let's say the example year would be 5%. This amount was relayed to the department heads. Then the skullduggery began.

At the PD we'd work out a budget with a legitimate 5% increase, then boost it by 10%. This was forwarded to the City Manager as a 15% requested increase.

The City Manager, to do his job as scrupulous guardian of the public funds, would study our budget and cut 5%. Looked good. He'd lopped off an amount before the budget was forwarded to the City Council for final approval. And we still had in it what we really wanted plus and extra 5%.

Next the City Council sweated over the proposed spending plan and, finally, after much deliberation, were able to cut off another 5%. That was 10% cut by the City Manager and the City Council.

The public loved it. And so did we. We got the 5% we really wanted and everyone was happy.

The games folks are sometimes required to play are, to my mind, unnecessary. One of my main problems was turning down officers and money we didn't need but the public clamored for us to accept.

EYEWITNESS TESTIBALONEY Cops learn early on not to rely--with certainty--on eyewitness testimony. In the police academy, a class is interrupted by some outrageous event. Say, a woman in a bikini being chased through the room by a fat man with a butterfly net. Stuff like that.

After things settle down, the recruits are asked to write down what they saw in as much detail as possible. *What happened? What they looked like? What they were wearing?* Keep in mind these are wannabe cops, with some training.

You wouldn't believe what they *saw.* Few can accurately described what actually transpired or what the participants looked like.

What's disturbing is that eyewitness testimony is some of the most compelling evidence you can present to a jury. They believe it!

Another exercise, to prove fallibility, is done by passing a short story around the room, whispered by one recruit to the other. Then the last listener tells what they were told. Again, it's nothing close to the tale that was started.

Something that started as "John Wayne was out riding on his Honda, drove over a banana peel, and slid into George Clooney who was pulling a rickshaw." This could end up "Marilyn Monroe bought a banana split from Humphrey Bogart who was working at a Dairy Queen in China."

No kiddin'.

That's why I could never choke down an Agatha Christie mystery or any of that ilk. The witnesses are so precise. *It was exactly 3:10 PM when I saw Fauntleroy stroll by wearing his blue, pinstripe jodhpurs. I know the time, because that's when I go out on my terrace each day to water my daffodils.*

Cops also soon learn that if they aren't careful, they can make a witness identify *anyone* else as the person seen doing a specific act. That's why photo lineups are so scrupulously crafted and witnesses are never allowed, before identification, to see suspects with the cops. *He's with the cops so he must be the one.*

Finally, white folks are just no good at even *attempting* to identify anyone but other white folks. Blacks, Mexicans, Chinese? *They all look the same.* A sad commentary but true.

Next, a case that showed me how easily this could happen in the real world.

EYEWITNESS TESTIBALONEY PART 2   A BOLO was out for one Jose Garcia. A bum check artist, he'd papered 5th Ave South, hitting almost every other store. That was bad news but there was a bright spot. Unlike many crimes, you can't pass a bum check without being *seen* and there were plenty of witnesses.

He was described as a "typical" Mexican male of medium height and weight, maybe 30-35. He was accompanied by a Mexican female, average height/weight, nod. And they had in tow about six head of children, all loud and irritable. Some folks had even seen his car, a two-tone 55 Chevy, black and white.

It wasn't long before our best birddog, Byron Tomlinson, had him in tow. Everything from the description matched. He had a wife and kids. He was driving a two-tone 55 Chevy. Three merchants identified him--through a two-way mirror as he sat in the interrogation room. This was gonna be easy. Except for two problems. We couldn't find any checkbooks and Jose adamantly denied that he'd written any checks.

We had, however, a good case, enough to allow me to take him to the CCSO jail and go home for the night. I'd just settled down for a episode of *Barney Miller*--the most accurate police show ever on TV--when the phone rang.

It was Mike Giddeon at the CCSO. Mike was doing a little of everything at the time, dispatch, crime scene tech, and jailer. Tonight he was a jailer.

"Think we may have a problem," he said. I asked what.

"I've talked quite a while with this Garcia fellar and I think he's telling the truth. I don't think he wrote any checks."

I asked Mike if he was familiar with the positive ID's, car, wife, children.

"Yep," he said, "but I think we have the wrong man."

Now Mike is one of the best cops I ever met and if it wasn't good enough for him, it damn sure wasn't for me. I saddled up and rode out to the SO to conduct a polygraph exam on Mr. Garcia to make sure. And guess what. He *was* telling the truth.

We started looking again. And found a *second* Jose Garcia the next day. A Jose Garcia who matched every element of the description: name, looks, wife, children, car. What are the odds of that happening in a small town (then) like Naples. A million to one? Who knows, but it's that *one* you have to watch out for.

The difference this time was, this Jose had a backseat full of checkbooks, and we convinced him to admit all his sins.

And, by the way, the same three merchants identified *this* Jose as the check writer, too.

ANCIENT PUNKING The first portable radios I ever saw in law enforcement were acquired by Sheriff Doug Hendry. We, of course, had them in the military but in law enforcement they were rare. Too expensive! But Doug, as he was apt to do, found a way around that.

The government had gotten in the Civil Defense business big time.

Don't recall who we worried about blowing us off the map at the time--or maybe it was for hurricane protection--but there were boxes of food, water and equipment available for any government official who wanted to put up with being the local CD Director. Doug checked into the program and found that portable radios were also available--free. So, he agreed to warehouse the food and stuff just to get the radios.

The things were just barely portable. We called them "lunch boxes" because they were about that size and as heavy as one stuffed with a thermos of RC Cola, ten Moon Pies, two cornbreads, and a quart of pinto beans. They were, however, capable of being lugged around and way ahead of anything else available for cops.

Over the years the technology improved. The walkie-talkies became a little smaller, enough that you could carry one on your gun belt without the weight pulling your drawers down. When Lyndon Baines Johnson learned how to rob the *Social Security* coffers and created the *Great Society*, even the NPD--under the LEAA giveaways--was able to acquire some walkie-talkies.

Chester Keene reminds me we'd also acquired a few parking attendants (meter maids) to patrol the newly installed meters at the "free" Naples beach. They patrolled in three-wheel Hondas.

One day Chester was on patrol and noticed a meter maid standing at the beach/street intersection, talking on her walkie-talkie. And he noticed she was holding her head at an odd angle, pressed against the radio, with its antenna pointing nearly horizontal, instead of vertical. She looked like Quasimodo trying to practice yoga. He had to know why.

She explained that she'd been having trouble with the radio, not ever having one before. She'd asked one of the patrol officers to show her how to use it properly. He told her to get the best signal you had to aim the antenna in the direction of the PD's radio tower. And she was twisting her neck like a bent nail trying to do it.

Chester, on the edge of erupting in laughter, and trying to hide it, explained that the contortions weren't really necessary. She could just talk into it normally. Then he went to *counsel* the before-his-time Ashton Kutcher that had punked her.

WINE AND CHEESE FESTIVALS Ever drive on one of our

new and beautiful four or six- lane highways and wonder why the speed limit is only 45 mph? Or why when you try to maintain the legal speed everyone on the road is blowing by you. Here's how it can happen.

Lets look at Davis Boulevard that was widened from a two-lane cow path to a real boulevard during my tenure at the CCSO. When new highways were built the standard way to determine the appropriate speed limit was with a procedure called the 85th Percentile study. The study required the monitoring, with radar, of the traffic on the new highway over a period of time, say a few months. Before the monitoring, a proposed speed limit was set on the road, say 55 mph.

At the end of the monitoring period, if the road being travelled had not had an above-average accident rate, demonstrating that it was safe at the speed motorists had been traveling, the speeds were analyzed. The speed that 85 percent of the cars were driving at is the 85th percentile and what the speed limit of the road should be.

That survey was done on Davis Blvd and the resultant speed was a little over 60 mph. Consequently, the Florida Dept of Transportation recommended the speed limit be 55 mph, just to be on the safe side.

Sound reasonable? Not in the Elephant's Graveyard. Not in the domain of *wine and cheese* government where a group of *whiners* can gather up a few *cheesy* elected officials and get what they want. In this case it was some folks from Kings Lake who said they couldn't drive at that terrifying speed (55). Or exit their sub-division safely--even though they had a traffic light. One resident told me in private that the real issue was they feared the high-speed "tire noise" would keep them awake. Yep, that's what he said.

And guess what, they got what they wanted--a 45 mph speed limit. I remember talking to the engineer on the project after the decision was made. "Don't you realize," I said, "that you're saddling the Sheriff with a constant enforcement problem. Drivers see this big highway and naturally speed up to 55 or 60. Then the Sheriff is supposed to write tickets where they're not really needed." The engineer just nodded and said it was out of his control.

So we've had a speed limit there that's about 10 mph under what it should be. Not just there, either. Ever check out Golden Gate Parkway? Get off the Interstate driving 70 and enter it--a highway that looks just like I-75. So, your speed creeps up and pretty soon you're getting a ticket cause the speed limit on *this* autobahn is 45 mph.

Go figure. But, if you're in *whine country*, don't bother with anything sensible like the 85th percentile study or your gonna be real disappointed.

THE NAKED PARROT CAPER   Roger Fussell, long time Deputy and Maintenance Supervisor for the Collier County SO, stocked a big stack of 4'x8' plywood sheets. For hurricanes? Nope, to cover door and windows openings after forced entries had been made to residences by the SWAT team and others.

When we blow open a home, we are responsible to secure it until the owner--now usually in jail--can tend to it. So Roger would board up the openings where doors and windows used to be before the rams and explosives did their work.

Entering a hostile environment, sometimes fortified, is very dangerous and we take the steps necessary to keep the odds in our favor. Such was the case one night in the mid-80's. We'll let Dave Johnson take it from here.

The Special Response Unit--what the public calls SWAT--was assisting Narcotics in serving a search warrant in East Naples. Unbeknownst to the Good Guys, the Bad Guys--who were long gone--had left a large parrot in the house. When SRU did the "knock and announce," the parrot started screeching. In Spanish. None of the Good Guys could *habla espanol* so they didn't realize it was just a happy *bird*, thinking his owners had come home. To the contrary, the Good Guys thought all the excited yammering was panicking Bad Guys trying to flush the goods.

With good reason for SRU to do what they do best--ram the door down, throw flash-bangs--they roared into the premises, screaming *POLICIA*.

Flash-bangs are concussion devices used to disorient. When they are tossed into an environment, a loud, deafening explosion--that usually blows out all the windows--and a blinding flash gets your attention in a hurry. As it did with the poor parrot, who proceeded to pull out all its feathers and then drop dead.

To top off the debacle, the Bad Guys had gotten hinky and moved the dope, so the Good Guys were left with nothing but a pile of bright colored feathers and a naked dead bird that they couldn't even eat.

The cops around the office started calling the SRU guys "Parrot Killers", which was pretty funny until the Bad Guy's sleazy Miami lawyer hit Sheriff Rogers with a lawsuit for way more than a parrot should be worth--except a gold plated one.

I think the Florida Sheriff's Association--our liability carrier-- settled that one with a fat check before the glue dried on the delivery stamps.

THREE WHEEL-GUNNERS AND A SEMI-AUTO SHOOTER

Pictured, from the 70's are Collier County SO deputies--left to right--*Robbie Kranz, Doug Nickel, Doug Caperton, and Tom Pomeroy.* Three have revolvers, the standard of the day. Pomeroy has a .45 semi-auto Colt, which were only allowed as a service weapon for a few who had demonstrated high proficiency with them.

Semi-autos have a propensity to "go off" unexpectedly. One CCSO deputy--carrying it stuck in his belt in the back like all the cops on TV and *few* in real life--tried to pull his weapon and shot himself in the azz. And a .45 makes a big hole.

GIDDYY-UP CLYDE   Several times the famous Budweiser Clydesdale horses visited the Collier County Fair. Always a crowd pleaser, the beautiful, majestic, equines, drawing the famous ornate wagon, were a highlight of the events schedule. Folks just loved them.

One year a deputy we'll call Humane Harry was assigned the overnight guard duty of the oversized oaters. The regular handler of the Clydesdales gave Harry a description of his watchdog duties.

"Most of the time they'll sleep standing up," he said, "but they have to sleep a couple hours laying down to get fully rested. Trouble is, sometimes they won't get up after they've been there a while. And if they lay there too long it can be dangerous, the weight and all. Just like an elephant. That's where you come in."

"Come in how?" Harry asked.

"You have to get them on their feet if they sleep too long."

Harry looked at the giant horses--some weighing over a ton--then back at the handler. "How the hell am I gonna do that?"

"I use this," the handler said, handing Harry a six-foot length of 2 by 4 lumber. "Just like you swing a baseball bat. Right on the ass."

"You've got to be kidding," Harry said. "I'm not gonna do that." And he didn't, walking off the job.

When asked by the Lieutenant, that assigned duty, why he'd abandoned his post, Harry replied. "First thing, I love horses. Second, who do you think the public would hang first if they caught me whammin' on a Clydesdale with a 2-by-heavy? Me or the Sheriff?"

His point was well taken.

Editor's note: Some folks--who know horses--tell me this story is apocryphal, that the handler had to be putting Harry on, that Clydesdales don't need special wakeup calls. I don't know. I'm just reporting what happened. And it damn sure happened.

GIDDY-UP CLYDE Part Two As often happens, a reader has come to my rescue. Cops and others who are familiar with the events that appear here, keep me honest when my facts are fuzzy. This time, Dave Johnson, CCSO retired, came to my rescue. And Dave said:

I have some info that might lend weight to this issue. I too drew the short straw a couple times, baby sitting those Clydesdales. It sure wasn't what I expected.

First off, the cute Dalmatian you see riding the Bud wagon in the Christmas commercials must've been on vacation. The one Bud sent to the fair was a black-spotted werewolf that would eat the ass out of your trousers if you looked at him sideways.

Second of all, when I was there our job was the same--make sure they stayed on their feet. If they laid down, we had to go get the wrangler--which pissed off the Dalmatian. Then the wrangler, grouchy because his sleep had been interrupted, would come out and wallop the horse on the ass with a 2x4 until it got up. Saw it with my own eyes.

The other thing people don't realize is that those elephant-sized horses erupt with methane gas clouds that would make a brontosaurus proud. So, you spent the shift walking around at eye-level with the behemoth's "nozzles", wondering where you'd left your gas mask. I can still see those bung holes opening up like Kodak apertures, followed by flatulent dust devils that would knock you to your knees.

The things a cop will do for extra money.

COLD SNAP In 1959 the newly formed Fair Board decided that we needed a county fair that was, each year, the *first* one in the nation. Don't know why, but it had to be the first. January. 1960.

And, being in the sub-tropics, that should be possible with our no-winter weather. So it was held at the old Fair Grounds on Radio Road, next to the old Swamp Buggy track and Stock Car oval.

Many Deputies and NPD cops worked the fair, some on duty, most off. And most of us spent our time huddled around 55 gallon drums that had been converted to emergency burning barrels to keep us warm. Why, in sunny south Florida?

Because you could bet your frozen hind quarters that a cold snap would come during the fair. And I mean a cold snap. No reason for it but predictable as skeeters in the rainy season.

The weeks before the fair could be sunny, beach weather--even for Crackers. (Yankee's will swim with penguins) After the fair, more weather like we were used to. But during. . .

It went on like that for years--with icicles forming on the children whirling on the rides in the frigid wind. Then, some other county decided *they* wanted to be the first--and coldest--each year and scheduled theirs a week before ours. That was a good excuse for the board to give up on the *first* thing and move the fair to February. Should be fine. Warm weather and still plenty of snow birds around to buy tickets.

Right. The fair is still in February and you can count on dragging out your long woolies during that week. Never fails. The cold snap follows our fair around like Obama dogs a loose dollar in your wallet.

Someone once suggested that they give up the whole winter thing and move it to June, or so, like most *normal* fairs. The idea was shot down. The Fair Board was afraid the attendant cold snap would kill all the crops.

HOOKER'S REVENGE There's an old joke about a preacher's sermon getting his holy-roller congregation so whooped up one of the ladies began talking in tongues, dancing, then rolling and somersaulting down the isle. At one point, her dress flipped over her head and remained there, exposing her gaudy red bloomers. And so forth.

The preacher, seeing her predicament, said to his flock, "May anyone who gazes upon Sister Bertha Mae, in her embarrassment, be struck blind."

To which the ol' Deacon, responded, slapping a hand over an eye, "Hell, I'm gonna risk one eye, anyway."

A few years back, some folks in Immokalee were risking a lot more.

The hazard came in the person of one Lucy Twattle. Lucy was a hooker in Immokalee back when AIDS was just getting a good start. Back then there were no medicines that would sustain your life and folks who knew about it were terrified of the disease. Or, they *should've* been.

Lucy was one of the first victims of AIDS. She was also the *Typhoid Mary* of AIDS in Immokalee. Lucy carried no condoms and *promoted* unprotected sex. There were always plenty of takers, men not being particularly enamored with "raincoat sex."

She plied her trade whenever she wasn't locked in the Immokalee Jail. Asked why she was deliberately trying to spread the death bug, she'd say, "That's the way I got it. Some sumbitch gave it to me and I'm gonna pass it right on."

Lucy quit showing up in jail after awhile. She either passed on or moved on, leaving a tragic wake.

EXCESS BAGGAGE Collier County has always been a lively smuggling port-of-entry. Rum, dope, people, we've had it all. Everglades City once got so notorious they had their own featured segment on *60 Minutes*. My pal, Chester Keene, has been in his archives again and dug out these memories.

When the developers decided we needed to dry up some of that nasty 'ol swamp and build a new community called *Golden Gate* it was a bonanza for drug smugglers. Many new roads were paved in remote areas of the

Glades. Roads that served little use except as landing strips for aircraft bringing in tons of marijuana. And other stuff.

Sometimes, with bigger aircraft like DC-3's, the pilot would drop below the radar, and do a touch-and-go on the road/airstrip. While he was taxiing on the runway his crew would be rolling bales of grass out of the plane. By the time he lifted off the plane was empty and he was back on the radar, seemingly just a dropout blip for anyone who was monitoring.

Waiting for this illegal bounty were vans and motor homes that were loaded to capacity and sent back to civilization. This only took a few minutes. And was hugely profitable.

So lucrative that some planes were just dumped after they were landed and unloaded. There was that much profit in the drug/marijuana import, a discarded plane just figured in as part of the overhead.

Pictured are two of these planes that Chester came upon. Just dumped and forgotten.

THE OTHER BARNETT Scott Barnett, an old friend and veteran cop with the Collier County SO, recalls one of his early arrests. As he tells it. . .

In the Spring of 1980, I was a recent graduate of the Police Academy and, now free of a Field Training Officer, on my own. I was on a solo midnight shift in District #6 (Marco/Goodland) when I was dispatched to a bar fight at the *Little Bar* in Goodland--a small fishing community off Marco.

Pulling into the parking lot, I could see a huge man inside the bar take a swing at one of the other fishermen. Knowing my nearest backup was at least 20 miles away, I went in, riot stick in hand.

I found the combatants out of breath from fighting. Busted-up around the bar were tables, chairs, and a few patrons. The bartender, pointing at a commercial crabber--we'll call Crabs Mash--said, "He started it."

This riled Crabs, who I feared was about to renew the mayhem. I quickly eased him outside. There, he calmed down, and I was eventually able to convinced him he'd have to go to jail.

I was glad he was compliant. The man was a giant. To give you an idea of his size, when I got out my handcuffs, to shackle him, he started to laugh. Thinking he'd changed his mind and I was either going to get my clock cleaned or have to shoot him, I asked him what was so funny.

My *almost* prisoner held out his wrists and said, "They don't fit. I've been arrested before and they tried. Won't go around."

Looking at his fence post wrists I had to agree. There was no way the cuffs were going to encircle them. Reluctantly, I told him go ahead and get in the back of the car. But, he wouldn't fit.

We were driving compact cars, Plymouth Volaries, and with the cage he couldn't get in the back seat. Knowing that there were only a few other deputies on duty in the whole county and none were driving anything bigger than I was, I asked Crabs if he would be good and sit in the front seat. That, or we'd have to wait for hours for someone to show up with a bigger vehicle. He agreed, barely able to even fit up front.

About half way to the Naples Jail, Crabs asked me my name, then asked if I knew a city policeman also named Barnett. I made a non-committal grunt and asked why.

Crabs said. "A few years back, I got arrested at the *Anchor Lounge* for fighting with the Naples PD guys and this city cop, named Barnett, hit me over the head with a stick or flashlight. My head still hurts and I'm still waiting to play some catch-up with him."

It's a great asset for a cop to have a good memory. But, sometimes a *selective* memory works better. I told him I'd never heard of this other Barnett and couldn't understand why any one would want to hit him on the head--the nice, cooperative gent that he was.

After I booked him into jail, I called the other Barnett and asked if he remembered the incident at the *Anchor* and Mister Crabs Mash. He said he'd never forget it. Crabs was the meanest, ugliest, and wildest thing he'd ever run into. I told him Crabs remembered him, too.

So that's it. An arrest from long ago that has stuck in my memory.

Oh, yeah. The other Barnett?

His name's Ray.

He's my Dad.

BOLITA Back before Florida took all the sin out of gambling by going into the business full time itself, there were two popular lottery type games. One, was The Numbers, run by organized crime. The other was Bolita, run by homegrown entrepreneurs. The Numbers game became the Florida Lottery's *Cash Three* entry.

Bolita came to Tampa from Cuba in the 1880's and migrated statewide. To play, 100 numbered balls were placed in a paper bag and bets were taken on the number to be selected at the drawing on Saturday night. Traditionally, a woman grabbed the bag, pinching one ball, then tearing it out of the bag. Usually, someone just reached in.

Bolita was notoriously crooked. Sometimes popular number balls weren't put in the bag. Some popular balls had lead inside to make them sink to the bottom. Some were frozen, to make them easy to identify.

You are never going to legislate morality, so why waste the time? However, when the games got too crooked we moved in. One Saturday we were informed that a lady named Catherine was the bag man--*lady* in this case--for Naples. She would collect all the bets from Naples and deliver them to Ft Myers, where the operation was run. We put a tail on Catherine and, when she made her pickup and headed for Ft Myers, arrested her.

Now, it was alleged that the Bolita operation had been run for years by the then sheriff of Lee County, Flanders Snag Thompson. We told Catherine that we weren't interested in her and if she'd tell us who she was delivering the money to, we'd cut her a deal. She refused, obviously terrified.

We kept at her and she adamantly refused to reveal the boss. Seeing this wasn't going to work, we tried another carrot. We told her if she'd just give *her* boss' name--never hoping to get the top man--we'd work with her.

Finally, she blurted out, "Lord, no. If Mistah Snag found out I even do *that*, he'd be killin' me."

Catherine got probation. We turned the information on Mistah Snag over the the Florida Department of Law Enforcement. Although Snag was never convicted of running the Bolita operation, shortly thereafter he was removed from office by

Governor Claudius Maximus Kirk for a truckload of things a sheriff wasn't supposed to be doing.

AFTER THE PROM DATE Wanna know how cops got all the benefits? Pensions. Insurance. Decent pay. Wasn't because the governments were in the charity mode. I was because they *had* to do it.

Back in the day, cities and counties--especially in the South--couldn't hire cops. Why? No benefits, the was pay awful, the hours sucked and, oh yeah, you could get maimed or murdered. So, as an inducement, they gradually improved the salary and added the benefits. Otherwise, if you wanted to fill your roster you had to be inventive.

Take Dave Johnson, with the CCSO. When age 21 was the norm, Dave became a certified Deputy at age nineteen. He was hired at 18. He was so young, he had to leave his prom early to report for duty on the 11 to 7 shift that night. And not old enough to buy bullets. But, he's been a good one! Junior Deputy at first or not.

PIGEON DROP ALIVE AND WELL When I first made Detective, in the early 60's, the first con game I ever worked was the Pigeon Drop. In the news this week, is a sad story confirming that the ancient scam still works. Hard to believe, but true.

An octogenarian was victim to con game weasels, being relieved of a couple thousand dollars she could ill afford to lose. The poor lady is still working at WalMart to get by.

The game, always has the same elements; a wallet or whatever, supposedly full of money, found in your presence, and "earnest money" being put up until the money can be divided. The mark, or pigeon, gets to keep the money in their custody, finally realizing they've been stuck with an empty wallet.

Of course, it relies on the *pigeon* being greedy or, as above, desperate for money. If, when the money was supposedly "found", a call was made to the police there would be no scam. But the con artists are fast-talkers and experience great success with the game. And have for over 100 years since it migrated over from France.

Yep, makes you wonder how anyone could fall for such a stunt.

Course, when I was a juvenile delinquent in Charleston, WVa, we used to tie a string on an old wallet, leave it on the sidewalk and hide in the bushes. When someone bent over to get the wallet, we'd yank it back and run like thieves, laughing like maniacs. We were amazed then, too, at how often it worked.

GRADUATING CLASS JUNE 23, 1988

This photo is of four officers ending an era at the Naples Police Department. All had over twenty years of service and were soon to retire. The occasion was an award from the Optimist Club commending their years of devotion to the safety of the community.

Pictured are, from the left, *Richard Davidson, Chester Keene, Dave Dampier, and Barrie Kee.* Richard and Chester went on to also retire from the Collier County Sheriff's Office. Dave was very successful in the real estate business and Barrie really retired, but still devoted his time to his beloved Police Athletic League, of which he was a founder and prime mover.

LOUIS COLLINS In the old ballad *Louis Collins*, legendary bluesman Mississippi John Hurt bemoans the shooting of a young man and the grief it caused his family and friends. And what a waste it all was. He could've been singing about our Louis Collins, a young NPD officer who came to a tragic end years before his time.

Lou was home grown and tried several jobs Cracker's do before finding police work. He found he loved it and was good at it. He had almost a year on the job before he went to the police academy. That's where the terrible accident happened on December 3rd, 1971.

LOUIE COLLINS

The students were just returning to class and taking their seats. Although firearms were strictly forbidden in the academy classroom, the recruit sitting in front of Lou had sneaked one in. He had it in the back pocket of his bib overalls. When he started to sit down, the pistol--an ancient S&W top-break .38--fell from his pocket. Being an old gun, it had no *hammer block*, or device preventing the gun from firing if it was dropped and hit on the hammer.

The gun went off. Lou grabbed his chest and said, "My God, you've killed me," and fell to the floor, instantly gone.

His name appears on the *End Of Watch Memorial* at the NPD.

We still miss you, Brother.

Choir Practice
Session Nine

J.D. IN HEAVEN One could say the Almighty had gotten out his digital camera and snapped this photo of JD Spohn lounging behind the Pearly Gates, showing everybody how it's done. Anyone that had the pleasure of having JD for a friend knows it's true.

This is surely how he would have wanted it. Cowboy hat, boots, camper, BBQ, and toddy in hand. And those trousers look like he may've not had time to get completely out of uniform before it was party time.

Not enough guns for JD Spohn, you say? Just one on the right hip. Better check them there boots. And his pockets. And under that hat.

Miss you every day, old Poddner. You were a true original and I don't expect to encounter your like again.

"Wait a minute," some of you may say, "what makes you so damn sure JD's even in Heaven?"

Oh, he's there all right. Talked his way in.

This photo courtesy of ace photographer and archiver Chester Keene

A HORROR STORY The recent hullabaloo in the news about the deficiencies in our education system caused me to ponder. And that's always a dangerous thing, usually resulting in a rant. Here it is.

Back in the 80's the State of Florida decided that every police

146

applicant must pass the TABE test. That's Test of Adult Basic Education. The test had been developed in the 60's to see if you'd learned enough in high school to meet the standard of what a graduate should know. Passing score on the test was 12th Grade Level. By the time it got to the 80's the failure rate was so high, the passing high school equivalence had eroded down to 9th Grade. That's a Freshman in high school.

When we began giving the test we were astounded. There was one group who consistently passed it and another who couldn't get past 7th grade. The successful group was usually folks in their late 40's and up. The group that couldn't buy a passing grade were recent college graduates.

That's what I said, recent college graduates. And not from these dubious towers of learning like Edison State College and the their ilk. These were people with sheepskins from state universities.

The situation got so bad that when one of these scholars applied we'd tell them to go to the book store, buy a study manual for the GED test, and concentrate on English and Math--the two killer areas for college grads. Most were glad for the help after they'd taken the test. It's been so long I've forgotten all that stuff. Right! Four years.

So we started slippin' and slidin' on this slope a long time ago. And I'm not blaming the teachers, which is the popular thing to do. I'm wondering who's providing the curriculum they are required to teach. And, worst of all, how any teacher can deal with the chaos that's allowed to go on in classrooms today.

We'd better make some changes. Our education level is in the bottom tier worldwide.

THE POLICEMAN'S BALL Although I joke about Naples in the old days, and some of the funny things that happened, most of the time we got it right. And, in the process, built a great place to live. I wouldn't live anywhere else, and I've been around and seen what others have to offer. One of the things the NPD got right every year was The Policeman's Ball.

We started it as a way to raise money for the kid's program, PAL. And, because a Policeman's Ball is a traditional get-together. We'd hire one of the old dance bands: Glenn Miller, Tommy Dorsey,

Harry James, big names like that. Course, Glenn and Tommy and Harry were long gone but the music had been inherited by one of the band members.

The first time I was involved in the hiring, the night of the ball one man showed up. He said he was the "Glenn Miller Band." Had been a actual member and owned the "charts", the original arrangements. I was terrified at the aspect of waltzing this dude out and claiming he was the band.

He laughed. "The band will be here directly," he said. "I hire union musicians out of the Miami local for shows in South Florida."

"But, can they play like Glenn Miller?" I asked.

He smiled again, "I have the charts. If you have the charts a pro can play them. I could sound like The New Ashmolean Marching Society and Student's Conservatory Band if I had the Charts."

And they did. Any band, every year.

The first time we held the dance, we had our officers carry tickets around and sell them. One officer was particularly effective. He was out-selling everyone. A big, intimidating man named Jerry, he'd go into a business, fan out a fistful of cards, and ask, "How many?" We had to tone his tactics down.

But, after the first dance, ticket sales were no problem. There was just no dance comparable to it in Naples. In fact, we had to limit the number of tickets so folks could fit in the venue.

Wonder why they don't still have them?

MARCO MYSTERY I once had a job that didn't allow me to tell folks what I did. Had to lie about it. When it ended, I had to sign a paper swearing I'd continue to lie about the work for 15 years. Under penalty of prison.

The job was on Marco Island. Back then--the early 60's-- there was no bridge by the Isles of Capri. You drove down US 41 to Royal Palm Hammock, turned right on CR 92, and went over the swing bridge at Goodland to get to Marco Island. A long haul.

At the bridge there was an entire frame house roosting in the trees on a small island. It had been blown over there by Hurricane Donna. Took it years to rot and disintegrate.

On the other side of the bridge was a small blue and white motel where tourist fisher-people stayed. Johnny Unitas and other Baltimore Colts loved to stay there. Some said Johnny actually owned the motel. I don't know but he sure spent a lotta time there.

The fishing then was like no where else on earth. It was impossible not to catch something--many times one worth sending to the taxidermist. There was a 10' wide channel next to Caxambas that, each spring, was the highway for tarpon heading further north along the Gulf coast. They went by for several days, a solid silver highway. We used to wade out to the center--it was only about 4' deep--and stand in the middle of the stream. The tarpon ignored us, just making a wider path to get around. They would neither stop or eat. There were thousands. An old Cracker who'd lived on Marco all his life (he'd never been further North than Ft. Myers) said they'd done it each year for as long as he could remember.

To finally get to work, we'd drive to the Caxambas Pass where the government had bought the entire point and fenced it in. There was a guard at the gate. Several buildings had been constructed, one with two huge radar dishes on the roof. And there was a 300' communications tower. We'd go inside the buildings and prepare for our day's work.

We were working on the first man-space program, Project Mercury. The one where they put Sam Shepard and all those brave folks into orbit in an Atlas missile. That's what we told folks, anyway. And it was partially true, we did do that--about every 90 days. It was what we did the other 89 days we had to lie about.

MORE MARCO MYSTERY We would car pool for the trip to Marco Island each day. About twice a week, when we drove through Naples, Fred Scott, an NPD cop, would pull us over. "Where you boy's say you were goin'?" he'd ask. Fred's cop's nose told him there was something about our Project Mercury story that stunk.

When I got in the cop business, Fred and I became good friends. He'd still ask me about the tracking station job but, he died before I was allowed to tell him the truth.

There were seven tracking stations like ours stretched from Eglin Air Force base to Key West. We all did track the Mercury capsule with our giant radars, locking on it when it cleared the coast of

California and losing it in the mid-Atlantic. We also tracked the U-2 that secretly flew over Cuba, checking on what type of installations they were building. Like the ones that eventually led to the Cuban Missile Crisis.

But what we did most was called electronic counter-measures. This was new technology at the time and involved trying to avoid missiles that were trying to shoot down our missiles. And we're talking about missiles not carrying astronauts but nuclear warheads.

The company we worked for was called Vitro. But we really worked for the Air Force. Had to have a high-level secret clearance to work there.

The Air Force would launch a rocket from Eglin and we'd try to track it. It wasn't always possible, since the missiles had on-board electronics that put out signals to deceive any tracking radars. We'd usually end up tracking a ghost image while the missile went on it deadly way.

Actually, the missiles dropped harmlessly into the Gulf south of Key West. And the warheads were dummies.

The two radars we used for tracking were impressive. They put out a million watts, each. The computers that guided them were contained in fifty floor-to-ceiling cabinets. This was before transistors and glass diode tubes were used. Thousands of them. To make a repair, you got a schematic book-there were forty of them-- found the likely cabinet, then the defective tube in the racks. Not easy. This early computer had less computing power than the little Radio Shack Color Computer I later owned.

So there it is, the Marco Mystery solved. If you even knew there was one.

DOUBLE TROUBLE Many of the officers at the Naples PD had so much fun in the cop business that, after they retired, they went to work for the Collier County Sheriff's Office. They were, after all, still young and could work long enough at the CCSO to get another retirement.

It was a good deal for both. The cops got an easy transition into an agency they already knew and the Sheriff got Deputies who were experienced, trained, and proven veterans.

A few Deputies, went the other way: from the CCSO to the NPD.

Chester Keene was one of them. Chester, after doing the two hitches, still had enough energy left over to give me considerable assistance with this book and write an occasional article in the Naples Daily News.

Another was Ken Ferrell. Ken did his time and now, never tired of risking his life, climbs mountains. Or runs up them. Pike's Peak, stuff like that. He also works at The Phil.

Pictured above left is Richard Davidson. Richard went from NPD to CCSO to security at Naples Community Hospital. I heard he was still working there.

Then we have this poor, young, innocent soul. He climbed through the ranks to Chief of Police, then Naples City Manager, then moved on to the CCSO. I understand he's still there. What was his name? Oh yeah, Rambosk. Kevin Rambosk. Sheriff Kevin Rambosk. *Photos 1985*

DOUBLE TROUBLE, TOO There were other Cops who worked for both the Naples Police and the Collier Sheriff's Office: Ray Barnett, Richard Cooper, Dave Lester. There were many more that migrated from the PD to the SO than taking the reverse path. Probably with good reason.

The NPD was notoriously strict and would fire you in second. That applied to the Chief right on down. The SO had a much more forgiving nature. Hell, you'd have to be caught red-handed holding up the Bank of Naples to get a reprimand. There was a reason for that. Disgruntled Deputies were bad politics. Their grumbling could cause the loss of many votes.

Also, the CCSO was larger and growing. There was much more

opportunity. And there was the other thing.

At the time, the SO had a deal with the current Chief that neither would hire the other's officers. Before an officer would be interviewed, they must have notified their boss they intended to apply. This scared many off. What if I'm not hired? The Sheriff/Chief will fire me for being a traitor.

The city kept the agreement. The SO did not. Not even close. Unless it was someone they didn't want anyway. Then it was We can't process you until you tell the Chief you're applying. We knew of several cops they actively recruited. If it was a prime candidate, we found they had already been guaranteed a job before they came and told the Chief.

Ray Barnett had been a cop in State College, Pa. before the NPD. He was one of my first Detective partners and is still a close friend. Ray, smart, smooth and a great cop, rocketed to the top at the CCSO, finishing off as a Chief. He later went into the private sector. Our loss.

Dick Cooper is one of my favorite people, also a good friend. I hired Coop to work in the jail after I went to the CCSO. He was a great street cop but he figured the chances for advancement were greater in the rapidly growing jail section.

One sad day, a cowardly scumbag inmate, who should have been in state prison, attacked Coop and smashed his head into a heavy steel table. Coop nearly died.

When his body healed he had to rehabilitate his mind. He'd lost the ability to read, and count, his memory destroyed. But, Dick, one of the toughest out there, pulled it off. Besides his tenacity he had another asset: his wife Josie.

GEORGE   Knew a kid once named George. Knew him from the time he was about six until he graduated high school. George played for the PAL Gators football team and he was one of the best running backs I ever coached. Almost impossible to take down.

Since George was the same age as some of our kids, he used to, occasionally, come up and stay at our house in Pine Ridge over the weekends.

Getting permission from his parents wasn't necessary. George didn't have any. George was raised under the system that has evolved in many Black communities where a kind-hearted lady will take in children who have been abandoned. Cast aside. Forgotten in favor of booze, dope, and trips to The Clubbb. They are usually called Grandmas or Aunties. May God love them.

George, being black, lived in the Naples' shameful hellhole called McDonald Quarters. A ghetto. One of the few places Blacks were allowed to live in paradise. George survived this meager existence with amazing resilience. He was healthy as a horse. His sense of humor fine-honed and ready.

Once when George was staying with us, I noticed that he wouldn't jump off the diving board into our pool. I asked if he would like me to show him how to dive. George said, "Oh, I can dive just fine. Just don't think I should."

When I asked why he said, "When I starts bouncin' on that board and I bounces higher than that fence around the pool, your neighbors gonna see my black ass. Then they gonna say 'Uh-oh, lookit what's bobbin' up over there' and you gonna be in big trouble."

George once told me something that caused me to re-think many things I took for granted. He seemed to like staying with us so much that Sandy and I had discussed trying to get custody of him. I asked him if he liked visiting us. "Oh, yeah," he said, "an' you know what I like best? I love sleepin' in a bed on Friday and Saturday nights?"

"What do you mean?" I asked, confused.

"In the Quarters you can't sleep in a bed on Friday or Saturday nights. They gets drunk and starts shootin', you best be sleepin' on the floor so them bullets pass right over you."

Being a cop I knew he was right. But I'd never thought about it. Why should a kid have to worry about things like that? And not just him, every kid over there. But, it was just a fact of life to them. After that, we tried to make life there safer.

We finally lost George. One of his Aunties found a relative up in Mississippi and George moved there. Did well, I understand. Went on to play college football. A big running back that couldn't be stopped.

YOU WANNA BE A WHAT? When Dave Johnson, Sarah Creamer, and I were the Personnel Section at the CCSO, we interviewed and tested countless applicants. And we encountered some strange ducks. Folks that made you wonder why they came anywhere near a cop shop.

While we were doing the background investigation on one such buffoon, we found there was an outstanding felony warrant for his arrest. So, the next time he came in, we made him an offer he couldn't refuse. A position in our jail. Behind bars.

We discovered another, a cop in Denver, who'd also been one in Hawaii. Using another name. This genius was bagged when he got confused and provided us with training certificates under the second name from Hawaii instead of the ones from Colorado.

Then there were the "disabled" cops from up north. Most of these were from New York, with an occasional thief from New Jersey. Now, don't get me wrong, we hired many cops from the NYPD. Great cops, take all of them we could get. But, the NYPD has to be the bogus disability retirement champ. Especially, the PD and the Sanitation Department.

We'd regularly interview dudes who said they were retired on the "disabled" list. Some would give us a wink, like we were in on the scam. Then, when we'd explain that we couldn't hire a disabled person to be a street cop, they couldn't understand. But, I'm not really disabled. Some demanded to take the physical fitness test to prove it. They just didn't seem to understand that they were criminals and we arrested crooks, we didn't hire them.

We caught several in related scams. Perhaps the worst was a NYPD cop who, when off-duty, slipped on a curb at his home and broke his leg. Not wanting to miss a chance that it might be a career ending injury--and eligible for a disability pension--he nursed the broke flipper until the next morning, drove to work, then "tripped" getting into his patrol car, breaking his leg. And, need I say it? It was New York and he collected.

Didn't I read recently that the New York retirement system was broke? Wonder why?

YOU WANNA BE A WHAT? PART 2 The parade of applicants that should've shunned police agencies like politicians avoid common sense continued. Some of these clowns must've thought that law enforcement experience preferred--in the advertisement--meant having a criminal rap sheet.

Once, when the CCSO was hiring a load of Deputies, there was such an influx of folks with warrants pending that a special system had to be set up to process them. Criminal histories were run before any testing or interviews were conducted. When those with a confirmed warrant popped up, they were notified to report to the Duty Officer Desk and ask for a certain Sergeant. This Sergeant was a Warrants Deputy who would welcome them to the agency--so to speak.

Sexual activity gets a lot of us in trouble. But, the extent to which some of our applicants were involved, boggles the mind.

Several applicants admitted to having sex with animals, dogs being the unlucky preference. One minimized the act. It was just oral sex. And the dog didn't mind, he liked peanut butter.

Then there were the more prosaic--among applicants--acts of sexual abuse: sex with minors, rape, date rape using drugs, child porn. When these was admitted by locals, an investigation was conducted and when the crimes were confirmed a warrant was prepared and, you guessed it Welcome To The CCSO.

For out-of-towners an information letter, with the admissions, was sent to their local law enforcement agency.

Ex-cops weren't exempt from the stupid list. One Chief of Police from a small town admitted to stealing over $20K from a drug bust scene. And he was proud that he hadn't been greedy, having shared the tainted proceeds with the rest of the 5-man force.

This resulted in a phone call to the jurisdiction involved, where an investigation caused the entire police department to be shut down.

Then, there were the imbeciles who told the Polygraph Examiner, when asked if they'd ever smoked dope, Not usually, but I did take a couple hits in the parking lot to level myself out for the lie detector test. (Yours truly is a polygraph examiner and I heard that one more than any other)

One of the champions in the weirdness poll had to be a couple from Miami. The man admitted to being a tranny who had been arrested for prostitution while being dressed as a woman and using a woman's name. His girlfriend, I suppose to kinda balance things out, had a male identity.

We decided to let them continue to reside in Miami where that lifestyle fit right in.

THE MYSTERIOUS SAFE For many years the offices of Smith-Lesher Insurance occupied the corner of 5th Ave So and 8th St, kitty-corner from the 5th Ave Rexall. A reputable, respected company, it was remarkable to us in only one respect. The huge safe within. And what was in it.

Judge Harold Smith was the cause of this wonder. He'd left orders that in the event of any criminal attack on the property he was to be notified immediately. Burglary, armed-robbery, larceny, anything. Particularly, if it involved the safe. He would never tell us why he had this vested interest. (He wasn't the "Smith" in the agency name, that being the ex-mayor Roy Smith family.)

Once we had occasion to call the Judge. There was a B&E and the office had been ransacked to some degree. There was no indication the safe had been violated. And being built like a Sherman tank, we would've been surprised if it had. It was a monster, of superior quality, and would've tested the talents of Willie Sutton. These burglars were of the smash and grab variety, not possessing such talent. But we called Judge Smith quickly and he promptly arrived on the scene.

Judge Smith told me: "I'm going to open that safe. I want you to stand behind me, with your back to me. I want you to insure that no one looks into the safe, including yourself." He than went to work, from the sound of it shuffling papers for about 15 minutes. Then it was over. "We're okay, here," he told me. Then turned to leave. "Oh," he added, "leave this part out of your report." And we did.

We did know that Judge Smith had had some ties to military intelligence. And that he was on the list of folks to contact in case of a national emergency. But, if this was some high level government intelligence material he was guarding, would he put it in an insurance office safe in the Elephant's Graveyard?

The secret died with Judge Smith. And whomever else had the combination to that safe.

Thanks to Dave Dampier for additional facts.

THE NEW YORK SECOND The famous New York Second memo shows how Sheriff Hendry solved a personnel problem in 1975. Doug didn't even allow them the famous New York Minute--a second was enough.

SHERIFF'S OFFICE
Collier County
NAPLES, FLORIDA 33940

OFFICE AND JAIL 774-4434
P. O. DRAWER 1277

E. A. DOUG HENDRY
Sheriff

March 5, 1975

TO ALL EMPLOYEES:

Effective this date each and every person working for the Collier County Sheriff's Office will put in their eight hour shift and there will be no overtime paid, since there is apparently some argument about it. I worked hard on this budget to get it passed to where you would get additional pay and apparently some of you think you are trying to run the department.

When election time comes, the Clerk of the Court will take your qualifying fees to run for this job the same as she takes mine, and if you want to try me for it, let it rip, but I cannot say that I am going to run because every month I have got to enter in a report turned into Tallahassee but I believe each and everyone of you can read between the lines. As long as I am where I am in this position, there is nobody in this department that is going to try to tell me how to run it.

This was worked out to benefit everyone, to help supplement your salaries, to feed your families, and look after you. If you want to question it, read the rest.

If anyone wants to question me on it, or try me, I can have a replacement for you in a New York second.

I hired people to do a job, not to be a bunch of clockwatchers, and if I find out that anyone of you are not doing your job, then it will be just like the paragraph above.

Anyone that wants to question this action can hit the hard road.

E.A. Doug Hendry, Sheriff
Collier County, Florida

Dave Johnson says: I remember the day the NY Memo came out. Everybody messed their drawers. Those were the days when Doug could still manage to make the earth tremble. Not one bit of grumbling was heard after that memo. Not even whispers. All those that were griping shut the hell up and stayed out of Doug's line of sight.

The phrase New York Minute originated in Texas where folks said life was so fast paced in New York that they do in a instant what a

Texan would take a whole minute to do.

AN ILL WIND Read in the Naples Daily News about Paris Hilton being tripped up by the pungent odor of marijuana trailing from her limo. This caused me to remember problems the NPD and CCSO had with the stinky locoweed.

We first encounter difficulties after a drug bust, by the NPD, had yielded a substantial cannabis haul. Back then the courts required you to keep all that was seized, not just photographs and a representative sample.

It's aways difficult to find a suitable place to store the stuff. Because of its odor, even when sealed in plastic, the evidence locker can become fouled by the stink quickly--especially in large quantities. If you store it off campus, you have a security problem. Once the CCSO had a rented warehouse broken into and several bales swiped. So, we tried to get rid of the grass as soon as possible.

The best way to do that is to burn it. And there are those doobyphiles in the community that readily agree. The first time we burned a big load, we notified the Naples Daily News and other media sources so the public could see how productive our drug enforcement efforts had been. Told them we were going to burn the contraband at the City Dump. Even listed when. Bad mistake.

On the day scheduled for our pungent pyrotechnics, the dump was unusually busy. Every "head" and hippie in town was waiting, hoping to get downwind and a free high. And they did!

After that we tried to keep our burns secret but forgot there was normal dumping traffic at the site and word spread quickly. Even some of the workers there seemed to, coincidently, find their duties took them downwind of the yellow-green cloud. When the cops working the burn started getting all mellowed out, and calling dispatch after the burn with, "Hey, dude, I'll be 10-8ish" we knew a change was in order.

That's when we started hauling it by the truckload to the Tampa incinerator. Don't know it they still do that but when returning from Tampa recently, I could see the incinerator's stack to the West, puffing a peculiar yellow cloud. And the inordinately large flock of birds around it seemed to be flying upside down.

AN ILLER WIND Chester Keene reminded me of another attempt we made to burn our giant marijuana evidence holdings that went awry. Since way too many folks were enjoying whiffing the yellow-green clouds, at the dump, and our cops were getting as stoned as gooney birds trying to burn the stuff and keep the crowd away, we decided that if we could burn it faster the problem might be solved.

So at our next bond fire we soused the pile with diesel fuel. The diesel should accelerate the blaze and take half the time to turn the evil weed into harmless ashes. Plus, there was the added benefit that the diesel would ruin the smell the "heads" so enjoyed. That being the plan, a five-gallon can of diesel fuel was emptied over the pile and then it was ignited.

A ball of flame like a mini Hiroshima boiled skyward and soon the MJ was fully ablaze. We thought.

The disappointed crowd had moved on, the pile seemed on its way to extinction, so our cops went home. We found out later that as soon as we left the premises, some of the dump workers doused the fire and hauled off the considerable remainder to attempt to restore it to its former stupefying glory. And they did. Kinda.

For weeks after, the air in certain car interiors, bars, and bedrooms was tainted with the familiar wet-weed stink of burning "grass." And the gas station aroma of Number 2 Diesel.

Strangely, most tokers liked it. One doobie-puffer said it got you just as high as the unadulterated version, plus you got an extra ten miles per gallon.

VOLUNTEER DESTRUCTION TEAM Although the Naples Airport was not contiguous to other City property, it was owned by the City of Naples. Accordingly, it was patrolled by the NPD. We'd take a long loop around, well into the County, to get to the distant cousin of Amenityville.

One late night I was taking the tour and on arriving at the airport noticed a glow in the window of the small terminal building. (At the time it wasn't much larger than a residence) Looking through the jalousie door I could see flames. Not having a key, I pried up a jalousie and, in my best burglar fashion, pushed in the screen and turned the knob from the inside.

Once in, I could see flames coming from a waste basket. I extinguished the fire with a couple cups of water from a nearby cooler. There being no apparent cause for the fire, I called dispatch and told them to make the Naples Fire Department aware of the blaze in case they wanted to investigate. But, that as far as I could tell the danger was over. About five minutes later bedlam broke out.

Then, there was only one full-time fire department in Collier County: the Naples Fire Department. The other communities were serviced by volunteer fire departments. The volunteers did a good job considering they had little training and inferior equipment. But there are always some clowns out there.

One such circus-on-wheels had been monitoring our dispatches, heard the incendiary word Fire, and had decided to, well, volunteer. They blasted into the parking lot, siren screaming and emergency lights painting the scenery red. After skidding the dilapidated wagon up to the door, a crew of two men charged the door with a fire ax and began shucking the jalousies from the door frame. Then they uncoiled a hose and began spraying the inside of the building. I hastened to end this debacle.

"Why the hell did you bust out the jalousies?" I asked. "The door was unlocked. And why are you spraying? There is no fire."

One volunteer looked at me, then at the building. Then back at me, then at the hose. "SOP" he said.

Soon I convinced them to get the hell out of there and they rolled up their hose and departed.

The fire caused no damage. The volunteers caused thousands of dollars worth with their water and fire ax assault.

And for some time after, whenever I lit a cigarette I looked around to make sure these buffoons weren't in the area.

A NEW DANCE: THE ANCHOR FANDANGO A CVS Pharmacy has replaced the old Anchor Lounge on the corner of 3rd Avenue South and 9th Street (US 41). A logical choice--with their aspirins and bandages and all--considering the problems the Anchor caused the NPD. Of course, if you frequented the bar in the late afternoon, you'd noticed that several of the patrons wore a uniform of sorts:

spit-shined black shoes, dark blue trousers, and a Hawaiian shirt. These were NPD cops who'd just gotten off duty and had exchanged their uniform shirt for a sporty one so they weren't officially in uniform. But, many times their afterwork toddy was interrupted by the fisticuffs that were a featured attraction at the dive.

When we had only two cars on duty, and it was late on a Friday or Saturday night, you dreaded to get a dispatch to the Anchor. You knew it was a bar brawl and, more times than not, the other unit on patrol was out on a call and you were IT. Cops, to stay in one piece, become resourceful and learn to take their time going to a bar fight. If you can stretch your arrival five-minutes or so chances are when you do get there you'll find the combatants all "fought out"--puffing and blowing, and no longer interested in being a bare-knuckles champ.

That was most of the time. Sometimes that trick didn't work. One night, on arrival, we found a unique pugilist. A slight little man, he was on top of one of the tables doing a flamenco of sorts like a drunken Jose Greco. A crowd of rabid drunks circled the table, taunting the terpsichorean and trying to grab him. When one swiped too close, Jose'd add a step to his repertoire whereby his foot smacked against his attacker's jaw--knocking him cross-eyed.

My associate and I were so intrigued that we stood by and watched for some time, enjoying the show. We finally decided we probably should restore law and order before our dancer sent all the patrons to the hospital. When we approached the table, he pointed at us with his foot indicating "you're next."

The cop who was with me was large and ill-tempered when taunted. And he carried a huge leather slap-jack that could've been used in the World Series. He took it out and brought it down on a table, producing a sound like a pine being hit by lightening.

The erstwhile Greco immediately changed his mind and gave us a smile signaling "just kidding of course" and jumped off the table. We hustled him outside, took him to the cruiser, then gave him a lecture and had his friends take him home. Jail? No way. He'd been too much fun. And we might need him again to clean out another rowdy crowd at the Anchor.

WATERLOGGED Like the CCSO, the NPD has a long history of marine operations. In the early 60's, the boats were supplied by Outboard Marine Corporation (OMC), who had a test facility on the bay, just down from the NPD headquarters. The vessels were models they wanted to test and they figured the PD could put miles on them under all conditions. And we did.

OMC was a generous outfit. If you knew who to ask, you could buy boats, lawnmowers, and motor scooters--OMC owned Lawn Boy and Cushman--that had been lightly tested, for pennies on the dollar.

An additional benefit to the officers was that we were encouraged to use the boats for private excursions, family outings and the like. All that was required was that we paid for the gas. Most were reluctant to borrow them, knowing it takes experience to pilot a boat and even pro's could get into trouble. Once a Game Commission officer ran over the legs of swimmers near the pier. . .it was alleged.

After OMC, other builders donated watercraft to the NPD. The photo below shows Chief Paul Rebel and a sleek boat built and donated by Chincoteague Boat Builders.

WET WORK The Collier County Sheriff's Office has a huge expanse of water to patrol and respond to rescue calls. A Marine

Unit has been a longtime wing of the agency.

The photo below shows Sheriff Aubrey Rogers, and Collier County's second Marine Deputy Grady Johnson. With his back to the camera in marina owner Tommy Turner.

Grady, was a fixture in Collier County. His family were long-time local fisherfolk and knew the waters like none others. He could always be seen on or near the water. After he retired from the Collier County Sheriff's Office, he decided Naples was not the place he once knew and had outgrown him. He, and his wife Pat moved to Arcadia. Always a lover of politics, he decided to run for office up there and is presently a County Commissioner for DeSoto County.

On the next page, is Deputy Bert Morris. He was Sheriff Doug Hendry's first Marine Deputy. Bert, a veteran member of the agency, was last assigned as Commander of the Marco Island Sub-Station.

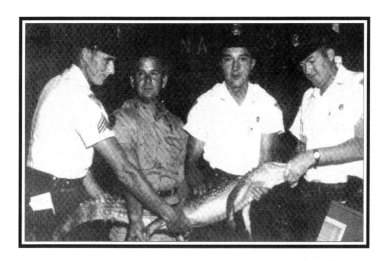

Caiman Catchers NPD 54

Left, Oran Coates, Unk game officer, Ed Helenek, Ralph Cox

Choir Practice
Session Ten

HIP-HOP CLYDE A gent we'll call Hip-Hop Clyde was a big man for the 60's era. About six-three, he weighed near 250. With his size came strength and amazing agility. They say he was also quite a dancer.

Clyde was a criminal from Ft. Myers who would visit us when things got too hot in the Land of Tom E. Fortunately, the visits were infrequent. Clyde was good at what he did.

What he did was crack safes and he did it in a unique fashion. His unique MO showed that Clyde had been there since few others could do the crime like him.

If it was an office safe, of the 250 to 300 pound variety, he'd just hoist it up on his shoulder and carry it home. If he couldn't comfortably do that, he'd use the method that definitely pegged him. He'd chop off the hinges with an ax, then pop open the door. Sounds impossible, but a durable, sharp ax in Clyde's hands was as good as a combination. I saw the results of his efforts twice. Clean cuts that looked like he hadn't taken more than two swipes on each hinge.

Clyde was hard to catch because first, he was a good thief, and second, he could run so fast. He'd outrun the cops in Ft Myers twice that we knew of and nearly dumped us one night off of 5th Ave No and the railroad tracks. If he hadn't gotten his foot caught in the ties, and yanked his leg off he would've. Yanked his leg off?

Oh yeah, that was the other unique thing about Hip-Hop Clyde. All his strength and athletic feats were accomplished by a man with only one leg.

Editor's Note: Chester Keene, after reading this, has added this verification.

Chester says: "When I was a rookie cop in Ft. Myers, I, along with another officer chased Ol' Clyde on foot down Booker's Alley. He hadn't been fitted for his wooden leg at the time and was on crutches. We were gaining on him when he threw down his crutch and outran us on one leg, pushing off the sides of the buildings and rebounding forward.

After he came to Naples. I saw him once on the street. He just gave me a Gotcha Boy grin."

RALPH'S MARVELOUS MYSTERY OIL We've mentioned Ralph Cox before, the former NPD cop who ran a private security patrol in Port Royal. And, we've written of Ralph's partner, the huge German Shepard Prince. After the sun went down 'til dawn the pair were ubiquitous in Port Royal patrolling in Ralph's cruiser of choice, a Morris Minor.

The Morris Minor was a shoe-sized, 4-cylinder British import that reminded folks of a malnourished '40 Ford. Small, uncomfortable, and about as appealing as blood pudding, they had little to recommend them. Except, like all Brit imports of the era, they were durable. Especially if Ralph Cox drove them. Ralph, you see had a system that allowed him to drive the toys up to 300K miles. That's 365 days a year. On the original engine.

Ralph would tell you that his key to long engine life was maintaining the oil. Nothing new there, right? Change it every 3 to 5,000 miles, use the best oil, filter. Nope, that wasn't it. Ralph changed his oil filter every 10,000 miles or so but never changed the oil. That's what I said, never changed the oil. He'd add to it, keep it topped up, but never drain and replace it. And he used the cheapest oil he could find.

"As long as it's slick," he'd say, "it'll work."

I remember he was torqued off when the reclaimed oil in bottles were taken off the market by service stations.

So there you have it. A field-tested program to save you money, eliminate aggravation, and extend your engine life. If you have the guts to try it.

I never did.

HEY SMARTY PANTS, WHERE'RE YOU GOIN'? Hiring for the CCSO allowed me to meet some very intelligent people. Some so smart that you had to make sure that all their furniture wasn't in one part of their attic. I'd worked with a guy like that on Marco, in the missile business. Waldo was brilliant . To a fault. His attic was chock-full of electronics knowledge. And not much else.

We worked shifts and more than once I encountered him in the parking lot, at shift change, with a confused look on his face. When asked the problem, he'd say, "Are we coming to work or going home?"

I liked to hire folks who were smarter than the average bear, but not too smart. One such, was recognized by his boss to be very bright and used to advantage. He was drafted to write for his boss-- who was trying to make Captain--a Master's Thesis. His boss, and the college, were ecstatic with the results. Hell, I think his boss may've even read it.

Another blazing beacon I took on aboard--who we'll call Grundig--was a pure genius. He was hired to do some technical work that required way more brains than muscle. Grundig fit the profile. As an example, he subscribed to a technical journal that was written in six languages. Grundig could read them all!

We did have a problem during the hiring process--I couldn't get him to bring in a copy of his Master's Degree. He would stall and make excuses, but never deliver. I finally put it to him: "If you don't let me verify your degree, I'm not going to hire you."

Grundig delivered it the next day. I asked him why he'd been so reluctant to let me see it.

"I was a failure and didn't want you to know," he said.

"Looks good to me," I said, noting the grades were all "A's."

"There is one A-minus," he said. "I was trying to get an all "A" college record."

The dreadful secrets some of us lock in our closets.

PHONEY PHONE CALLZ Scott Barnett remembers a story from the early 80's. He was a young, aspiring investigator then and anxious to get any experience in that line he could. Byron

Tomlinson and Ken Mulling suggested he participate in a drug bust planned for a duplex off what was then Kelly Road (Bayshore Drive) in East Naples. Scott jumped at the chance. As he tells it:

At 8 PM, ten of us gathered at the Sheriff's Office. I remember that Robbie Kranz, Wayne Graham, Harold Young, Mike Ryan, and Dave Johnson were also in attendance. Doug Nickel, who was lead on the case, described the building and curtilage, and told us where the drugs should be. Then, individual assignments were made for the raid.

Our plan in place, we traveled to the target residence in pairs, reached our assigned positions and, on command, went crashing into the house. All went as planned. Except, as so often happens in these well-planned intrusions, there were no Dopers present and no dope. I've found, over the years, that criminals have no consideration at all for the police.

Regrouping at the SO, our adrenaline still at an unrequited fever pitch, we decided there had to be other good work out there that needed to be done. Our devious intent focused on a slimball dealer in Golden Gate who we'll call Tony Fonzy. Tony had been giving everyone fits since he knew all the few undercover officers we had and, consequently, no one could make the required buys to put him where he needed to be.

Doug and Ken Mulling came up with a plan. Several of us were to sneak up and surround Tony's house, then radio back when we were in position. This done, Doug made an anonymous and urgent call to Tony. Out of breath, and seemingly panic stricken, he told Tony that the cops had just raided his friend's house he'd barely escaped. But, he'd heard the Deputies say they were coming to Tony's house next, so Tony should get the dope out of the house before the cops arrived with their search warrant and smashed down his door. Doug then hung up before any question could be asked.

In less than a minute, Tony's back door burst open and he and his girlfriend, an affectionate lass known as Catch Me, Hump Me, Hope I Trip, came running out with their arms full of dope. And right into ours.

A valuable lesson was learned that night. There's always more than one way to skin a weasel. If you're inventive. And not too particular.

BAUBLE BANDITS The jewelry business is notoriously shady. When you find a reputable jeweler, stick with them, because they can be rare. They're out there, but it might take some looking. Many a weasel lurks in the glare of a shiny stone.

One of the oldest scams, is the Free Jewelry Cleaning offer. Just bring us in your jewelry, leave it, and we'll clean if for you. No charge! Sound too good to be true? Well then. . .

This is what an unscrupulous thief will do. Give the stones in your jewelry a close inspection, identifying the superior ones. Then swap out these stones with fakes, or flawed ones. How do they get away with it? Most consumers can't tell the difference between a diamond and a dewdrop.

The weasels are always working. You can see them on TV every day. Most recent are the gold buyers. Mail us all your unwanted gold and we'll send you a check! Sure, but how big a check?

NBC news set up a sting on these scumbags. They had some gold jewelry appraised at a reputable dealer, then mailed it out to several TV gold buyers. The highest check returned was for 90% of the appraised value. Not bad. Then it went down hill, all the way to just 8% of what the gold was worth. This is just stealing your gold.

There are some who have little sympathy for suckers who get robbed by these crooks. They wonder why anyone would send their stuff off to some unknown grifter with any expectation of receiving full value.

If you want to sell your jewelry, go to reputable, local jewelers and get estimates. Even locally, you'll be surprised at the difference in appraisals.

Guess John Wayne said it best: "Life's hard, but it's a lot harder if you're stupid."

SLICKY BOYS An old scam is a good scam. Evidently. I recently overhead a cashier at a convenience store lamenting about being taken by what we called "Quick Change Artist", or a variety thereof. These scams are as old as prostitution but are, like that ancient evil, still alive and kicking.

These particular slick tricksters would hand a clerk a bill--say a

169

twenty--or receive it in change and ask the clerk to break it down as the con artist needed smaller bills. He might say "make it two tens." Then, as the clerk is getting the two tens, the request changes. "Go ahead and make that one ten and ten ones."

This isn't the exact language or "patter" but the intent is always the same: make the requests and changes so fast and often the confused clerk ends up giving the con artist more than he started out with. This is usually half, but sometimes is the whole twenty.

Sound impossible? Can't happen to you? If you encounter one of these fast taking dudes you'd better walk away or you could be next.

The quick change that required the most patience was the "dollar-splitter." We'd catch inmates doing this in jail cause they had a lotta time to waste. The required materials are a one dollar bill and a twenty-- or ten if that's the best you can do—some glue, and a very sharp razor blade.

The carver will start splitting the bills into halves, the front from the back on both. When the separation is completed, a hybrid is glued together, a twenty on one side and a one on the other. The bills are passed, of course, with the twenty side facing up. That's a potential of forty dollars.

Some splitters, who don't have the patience to do the entire bill, just take the corners that show the denomination. Then the bills are fanned like cards when passed, showing only the higher denomination number.

The things people will do to make a buck—literally.

BIG HEARTED JOHN Big John called me one day with a problem. "My new 'Man Friday'," he said' "Got a problem. Could you give me a hand?" I told John I'd be down directly.

Big John was the iconoclastic Gordon Drive millionaire of private zoo fame. We'd dealt with his Man Friday problems before.

John would hire a personal assistant to run his home, his domestic operation. All but his private zoo, which was his exclusive domain. His assistant would see that the home and lawn maintenance were attended to, the autos in perfect running condition, the groceries stocked, the laundry done, everything so John didn't have to worry about such trivialities.

In return, Big John was very generous. He'd pay a handsome salary, allow Friday to use the yacht, the cars, treat the house like it was his own.

Once Friday, when he asked John if he'd help him purchase a car, was pleasantly surprised. John bought him a Jaguar convertible, and financed it so Friday could pay him whenever he could. John was like that. To a fault.

So when he told me he had "Man Friday" problems, I knew what it probably was. Familiarity breeds contempt. Almost every Friday he hired eventually stole from him. And John would never prosecute, just let them slink away.

This case was the same deal, exceptional only in the depth of Friday's greed. On the books, the lawn service was being paid $500 a month, when the real cost was $450, the lawn guy kicking back $50 to Friday. The butcher charged $200 a month for steaks, which was 20% over the actual price, the extra kicked back to Friday. And so it went, with Friday jacking everyone he could. He even tried to get cut-rate newspapers off the kid that delivered Naples Daily News by threatening to switch to the News Press.

When I questioned him about his corruption, he came apart like a pair of Bangladesh sneakers, blubbering and whining about how sorry he was. This, of course, gave John just the excuse he needed to not prosecute.

We weren't done with this Friday. About a month later, John called me up. "Got a call from Friday this morning," he said. "Wanted to know if I'd give him a reference? What do you think?"

When I got done laughing, John said, "I guess that's a No."

That was Big John.

GETTING A HEAD PhotoShop is a relatively new program for manipulating photographs. It's difficult to view any media without encountering an example of its use. Movie stars not showing their age, amazing weight loss photos, you name it. Makes you wonder how we ever got along without it. Mike Gideon, retired Deputy from the CCSO, could tell you all about that.

If you were one of the Lost TV folks, stranded on a desert island,

Mike'd be one of the people you'd hope crashed with you. He's one of those inventive people who reflect the old American "can do" spirit. Don't have it? No problem. Give me five minutes and I'll come up with something. Mike could build a unicycle out of coconut husks.

Back in the 60's he had a chance to demonstrate his ingenuity. A moonshine still had been raided out in the swamp. Moonshine still? Yep, white lightening isn't under the exclusive purview of Appalachian Hillbillies. Cracker's can brew up a potent batch, too. And they used to quite often.

The CCSO had raided a large one out in the Big Cypress. It'd been photographed, dismantled, parts seized for evidence, and jugs full of shine hauled off or busted. Problem was, in their exuberance, they'd forgotten to wait for the Sheriff and Chief Deputy to get their photograph taken with the haul.

And it was a beauty. Just the stuff Sheriff's like to send out to the news media to show their constituents what a grand job they're doing protecting them.

But, fortunately for the Sheriff, he had the versatile Mike Gideon as a photographer. And Mike invented his own PhotoShop that day.

First, he found one of the moonshine still photos that showed Deputies posing with the evil percolator before it was razed. Then, he collected photos of the Sheriff and Chief Deputy of an appropriate size and angle, cut off their heads, and pasted them over the heads of the real Deputies at the scene. When he re-photographed his paste-up, you couldn't tell what skullduggery had taken place. The photo was never suspected to be a fake.

Oldies But Goodies

These old-timers are shown at a monthly luncheon meeting for the CCSO Alumni Association. From 2011 they are, left to right, *Tom Smith, Dave Johnson, Ben Caruthers, Scott Black, GD Young, John Hisler, Jack Gant, AC Edgemon, Sonny Lambert, Cathy Lambert, Robert Browning, and Larry White.*

These are the ones your mother warned you about.

Choir Practice
Session Eleven

A FRIEND IN LOW PLACES An attractive paradise like Naples has always been a haven for the rich and shameless. Captains of industry. Corporate heads. And, to the captains of other forms of skullduggery. Gangsters. Mafia chiefs--all "retired", of course. In truth, they were retired while living in Naples, adhering to the old mob adage "you don't crap where you eat."

One such baron of the bad guys we'll call Tony Bandana. Tony had been a kingpin in the Detroit Mafia. Some law enforcement agents, familiar with Tony's Detroit operation, said he ran the place. That no ongoing criminal enterprise in the Motor City survived without Tony's sanction and tariffs.

The FBI regularly visited Naples to keep an eye on Tony, parking near his house in nondescript cars, keeping track of the comings and goings--particularly when there were meetings with out-of-town-not-so-retired associates. In short, he was a major crime figure and it was no secret.

Ray Barnett remembers one afternoon, when Tony was at the Bank of Naples attending to his accounts. Leaving, he put his attache case on top of his Lincoln while he unlocked the door. And, like the rest of us sometimes do, he drove off, leaving the attache case at the curb after it slid off the roof. A good Samaritan reported the found case and Ray was called to the scene. He opened the case, to ID the owner, and was able to determine the owner was Anthony Bandana.

How could he miss. Inside were two, personalized, 8 by 10 photos of a couple of Anthony's admirers: Former President Franklin Delano Roosevelt and his Eminence the Pope.

THE SEVEN SHOT REVOLVER Bad Boy John Boom may've been the worse shot with a revolver in CCSO history. He was so inaccurate, when annual qualification time came Deputies tried to find out what time he was qualifying. Then make sure they were elsewhere.

You could count on him putting several of his shots into the targets on either side of his. And he once set fire to a blanket placed on the ground--to be used in prone position firing--by shooting a hot round into it. His gun was likely to go off at anytime in any direction. But, Bad Boy had other uses for a revolver. Dave Johnson remembers one.

As the story goes, one hoppin' Friday night Bad Boy checked out at a Juke, one of the finer establishments of the day off South Boston. He spotted a miscreant that was wanted for petty thievery and ordered him to come hither for some up close and personal

John Boom love.

The culprit declined and turned rabbit. Bad Boy started after him. Trouble was John was built like a kettle, not exactly an attribute of track stars. He knew he couldn't outrun his prey, so he pulled out his nickel-plated Colt Diamondback and, still at full gallop, started shooting.

Now, John had this particular habit that did not bode well for accuracy. He shot a revolver with a technique which resembled someone trying to sling something nasty off their trigger finger. Needless to say, John hit everything that night but the object of his intention. People and stray dogs scattered like flies.

Bad Boy, however, was not to be denied and, after his sixth and last shot, threw the empty revolver at the thief and brained him with it. He finished up the job with a few good licks of his trusty slapper, then hauled the desperado off to the jailhouse.

Only in Immokalee, only when Bad Boy was the Big Boss-Man.

Editor's Note: Bad Boy wasn't the only cop who found secondary uses for the tools of their trade. A Sergeant with the NPD and later the CCSO, who we'll call RD, was as accurate throwing a six-cell flashlight as an Aborigine with a boomerang. RD didn't like to run either and those who fled him regularly heard a whoosh in the air behind them--just before they were knocked silly--that wasn't the bird of paradise.

DIVORCE BAD BOY STYLE John "Bad Boy" Boom had other unorthodox talents that came in handy in the Immokalee ghetto. Ray Barnett remembers one of them. As he tells it:

After I'd left the NPD and joined the CCSO, I witnessed Bad Boy performing one of his famous divorces. He split the possessions-- better than any court--and told the male partner what he had to pay in child support, and when he could visit.

I was told that at times he would make them swear on his badge. The divorces were handled faster and better than the courts. And because they were a Bad Boy edict, no one with half a brain would violate them. Incidentally, there was no fee for the legal or medical services. This worked well, too, since his clients were usually short on the long green stuff.

We used a similar system in McDonald's Quarters in the City. When it became obvious that a couple needed to be separated before they separated each other via murder or mayhem, we'd divorce them.

The ceremony involved having them jump backwards over a broom on the floor. This voided a marriage that had been made by jumping forward over a broom, one of the "old ways" of doing it.

Then the cop, with fitting solemnity, would place his hand over his badge and recite, "By the power vested in me by the State of Florida, I pronounce you divorced." A return visit was seldom necessary.

A strange way to do business? It wasn't for all, but for those who believed in mojos, black cat bones, and possum pecker good luck charms it worked just grand.

BATTLEFIELD SURGEON Immokalee in the 60's was more labor camp than town. There were a few stores and decent homes but you didn't stray far off the main highway. Filth and squalor dominated the environs.

That's because Immokalee existed for farming--tomato and watermelon, mostly. And the product had to be picked. And that required hundreds of migrant workers--blacks at the time--who were herded up elsewhere by a "Straw Boss" and bused in. Here, they lived under conditions that made Naples McDonald's Quarters ghetto opulent by comparison: three and four families to a motel-room-sized hovel fit for a gulag.

Degradation, despair, and hopelessness are always fertile ground for violence and that was a prime crop in Immokalee, too. Cuttings, beatings, shooting were on each day's agenda. A murder was no more remarkable than the 98 % humidity or a sweaty shirt, sticking to your back, in the 100 degree heat.

Someone had to police this mess, and that fell upon the CCSO. The job required someone with particular talents. Although there were decent family types among the migrants, the roving, no-questions-asked lifestyle--like a carnival-- was a magnet for low-lifes and scumbags on the dodge.

The man selected to keep the lid on this garbage can was John Boom. Called Bad Boy. With good reason. A thick and gruff man, his reputation as someone you "bess not mess wiff" was well deserved. Bad Boy was fair and helpful--in his way--but demanded compliance to his version of law and order and had unique methods to make sure that happened. Today's FBI would've had to set up an Immokalee field office just to handle the civil rights violations he perpetrated.

Ray Barnett remembers being in Immokalee during the MLK riots. Still an NPD cop, he'd been loaned to help quell the violence. He was in the small Immokalee Sub-station, with Bad Boy and Immokalee Investigator Don McCarty, when an elderly black man stumbled in. His face was covered with blood. He went to Bad Boy.

Bad Boy inspected him, found the injury, and took out a pocket knife. Using it as a scalpel, he cut out a .22 cal bullet lodged between the skull and skin, poured alcohol on the wound and sent his patient home.

Ray gave McCarty a quizzical look.

"You ought to see what he can do with a needle and thread," McCarty said.

LET'S SUE SOMEONE! Once you retire and get a good dose of daytime TV, you discover there are some troubling constants. First, there's little on except "court" shows. Then there are the commercials, the majority pleas from slimy personal injury attorneys to sue someone. Everyone. Or collect Social Security you are not due. Or other dubious deeds that have caused these crooks to be held in such low regard. And I just read we have more than all the other countries in the world combined!

Now, let's get this straight. I have nothing against the legal profession. Some of my good friends are attorneys. People I admire that perform a necessary service. It's the weasels I have trouble with. The ones who make a living by suing every doctor, drug company, automaker--you name it--on ludicrous claims. Spilled hot coffee at McDonald's stuff.

I've being going to doctors for a long time and I can't recall ever contemplating a law suit for damages. Nor, can I think of anyone who has. This malpractice stuff is rare. But the manufactured fake claims support an industry.

It's no wonder drugs, medical care, and auto insurance cost so much. And Social Security is in jeopardy. Throw all these bums out!

Yep, I had it all figured out. Then, I read in the paper this morning that a federal study found that 1 in 7 Medicare patients are harmed in the hospital. That means either hurt or die from sloppy hospital habits. That almost 100, 000 die each year from preventable medical mistakes. That it cost us $4 billion in extended hospital stays. So much for malpractice.

Then, I remembered giving a polygraph test to a man we'll call Carl Candor. When strapped to a "lie detector" some develop a phenomenon called by cops "puking their guts up." They tell you the truth about everything. Even things not related to the issue in question. Things you don't care about. Carl was such a subject.

During the preliminaries, to calm him down, I made light conversation, asking him what work he did. He said he was an insurance adjustor. I asked exactly what that entailed.

He said, aware he was attached to a polygraph, "Well, first I try to screw the other company's client. And if that doesn't work, I try to screw our own."

So maybe we should thin the personal injury field down a bit. But not eliminate them, entirely.

FASHION STATEMENT?

This is the CCSO Criminal Investigation Division from the mid-1980's, probably about the time of the nationally famous Benson murder trial. Harold Young, in the center was the lead investigator on that case. For some reason the gang is all sporting "Clarence Darrow" type suspenders. Usually when something like this happened it was better off not to know why.

Pictured left to right, are *Mike Gideon, Bill Stiess, Scott Barnett, Jackie Kline, Jack Gant, Harold Young, Chuck Campbell, Tom Smith, Gene Brown, Mike Koors, Tom Storrar, and Dave Johnson.*

FASHION STATEMENT TWO   Chester Keene remembers a

morning when he was working in the Bailiff's Bureau of the CCSO. One of the Deputies had showed up for work in sunglasses. Seems they were required by his eye doctor because he'd had a minor procedure. He took his place in the jury box where all the other

Bailiffs were awaiting their court assignments for the day.

The Lieutenant, upon entering the room, spotted the glasses immediately.

"What's with the shades?" he said, "We all wear uniforms in this outfit. And they're called that for a reason. It means we are all dressed the same: uniform. Get it?"

The bespectacled Bailiff explained why he was wearing them and the Lieutenant responded with a non-apologetic grunt. This rude abruptness caused the other Bailiffs to suspect that their supervisor's personnel skills needed a little touching up. And they decided to do just that.

The next morning, at roll call, every Bailiff wore a pair of shades. And when the Lieutenant arrived he found, just as he had demanded, each Deputy uniformly attired.

The photograph of this fashion statement is above, taken by Chester whose vacant chair is visible in the middle. He said the picture would have been a little better but his shades got in the way.

LAST MAN STANDING Some folks that listen to my yarns give me a certain look. A doubting look. Anyone that can pile it that deep and keep a straight face oughta run for office look. These doubters are always civilians. Cops, who are usually the worst skeptics, are seldom surprised. They've seen so much the bizarre is common place. That said, I'm warning everyone in advance this one is going to be hard to swallow. But, it was related to me by Ray Barnett (right) while in the company of other old-timers who'd also been witnesses and verified it. So, here goes.

The "drunk tank" was a common fixture in all old jails. In smaller jails, where there were just a few cells, many times all the cells were designed so they could be tanks. The tank was an oversized cell, bare except for maybe a toilet, and a bolted- down iron bench or two. There was also a drain in the center of the floor.

A trip to the drunk tank put many an errant youth on the righteous path. One Saturday night of being packed in with filthy inebriates, who puked and pissed on each other--and you--did not beg for a repeat performance. Worse still, to get them all spiffy for court, some time in the early morning the Jailer would turn a hose on the lot, using the floor drain to dispose of the filth.

After one boisterous night in Immokalee, the little jail was packed full. Standing room only. Inmates clustered in tight packed groups, tighter than the illegal alien benefits line at the Social Security Office. When the door was unlocked, to sort them out, all passed out of the tank except one who stood alone for a second, then toppled over like a chainsawed pine. On inspection, it was determined he was dead. Signal-7. And, from his condition, had been for some hours.

Ray says that he can still hear Joe Cocker singing "I get by with a little help from my friends," every time he thinks about it.

DIVINE INTERVENTION Reverend Walter Lauster wasn't my preacher. I wasn't a member of The Church of God, on 10th Street North, of which he was the minister. Not a member of any church for that matter. Fact was, my relatives in West Virginia would've called me a backslider. Don't know if the good reverend knew that as he never asked my religious affiliation or anything about my beliefs, if any. That's one of the things I admired about him.

Our only dealings were tied to the police business--answering calls at or about his church. We did get an occasional call from neighbors about what they perceived to be an over- enthusiastic church service. I'm told Rev Lauster could shovel the fire and brimstone with great vigor but have no personal knowledge of it. I always found him to be a straight-forward gent who didn't try to save the world but might've been able to if he set his mind to it.

Those were the circumstances of our relationship. So I was mildly surprised when he showed up at my office, shorty after I was appointed Chief of Police, concerning a personal matter. He came right in, we shook hands, and he gave me my instructions. "Chief," he said, "we're going to kneel down and pray. I'll do the talking, you just listen."

I was really surprised by then and my face had to have shown it.

"Come on over here and kneel down," he commanded. "You may not realize it yet, but with the job you have you're gonna need some help." And his manner was such that I did what he said.

Turns out, he was right. And every few months, usually when I needed help the most, he'd seem to know, show up, and give me a "booster" prayer. I never questioned his visits. They just seemed a natural thing, like taking a handful of aspirins when you have a headache. Or a cool breeze when it's too damn hot.

Hope he knew how much he helped me.

Ray Barnett reminded me that I wasn't the only one he helped. "He helped a lot of cops and criminals and did it anonymously. He really practiced what he preached."

DIVINE INTERVENTION, TOO The Reverend was telling me his problems. We'll call him Reverend Most. He was pastor of a well-healed congregation in fat and frilly part of North Naples. Most was an acquaintance I liked to talk with. I didn't go to his church, either. Nor anyone else's. We never talked about religion.

"Problem is," he said, "the congregation thinks that I require a new car every couple of years. That either I do, or the wife. And they buy us one. Big, expensive ones."

"Geez, Most," I said, "that's awful. Wish I had your problems."

"I know," the Reverend said, "it sounds silly but it's awkward. Every two years a new Caddy or Lincoln shows up. And I still have the old one to get rid of. They never trade it in. I've told them I don't want a new car, but it does no good."

"Problem solved," I said. "Next time it happens, find yourself a deserving soul and exercise a little Christian charity. Give them the old one. Some deserving soul like a hard working public servant."

He laughed, and we moved on to equally frivolous conversation.

About two months later Rev Most gave me a ring. "How would you like to have a slightly used Caddy Sedan de Ville?" he said.

I was stunned, then remembered our conversation. "I was just teasing you the other day. I couldn't take something like that."

"And I couldn't give it to you," Most said. "But I could sell it to you at a heck of a price." And he did, doing both of us a favor.

It was a 1971 aqua Caddy, one of the big four-doors. And it was loaded. A honey. Sandy and I at the time were driving a Volkswagen Carmen Ghia that would have fit in its trunk.

But the venture was star-crossed from the beginning. I'll always believe the car had a mind of its own and knew it had been traded-down to drivers beneath its station. The problems started immediately.

It was 1973 and within two-weeks the phony oil shortage started. Gas shot up to prohibitive levels--if you could get it. And here we're sitting with a hog with an almost 500 cubic inch motor that was always thirsty.

Next, a visiting friend, backing out of our driveway and not realizing how long our parked Caddy was, bashed in the rear quarter-section.

Then there was the trip to Atlanta to visit Sandy's grandma, Big Mama. On the way up, we were nearly capsized when the left front tire blew off the rim. Before we got to A-Town, two more had done the same. (Radial tires were new at the time and less than perfect)

On the trip back, the automatic temperature control went goofy and wouldn't blow anything but cold air. And you couldn't turn it off. This was during a December cold snap with the air as frigid as GM's heart. When we got back we found the repair on the thing would cost a fortune. I went to Bob Taylor's Chevy and traded it in.

"Don't make many deals like that," Bob said. "Most folk don't trade in a Caddy for a pickup truck."

"Just goin' back where I belong," I told him, serious as a case of crotch crickets.

LUXURY PATROL CARS For a time, Ford owned a test track in Golden Gate. (Now owned by Harley-Davidson) It had a huge, paved, track and several shop-type buildings--the complete deal. And the Sheriff's Office was a grand benefactor.

Ford was looking for someone who could put miles on their proposed models and engines under rigorous conditions. Since no cars are more put to the test than police vehicles, we were a perfect match. So, they'd give us vehicles to test and we put them on patrol. It was a great deal for the taxpayers, but there were some odd caveats.

On some, we weren't allowed to lift the hood, look at the engine. Others, a Ford rep would supervise oil changes, maintenance, etc. The rules were understandable since Ford was trying to keep this info secret from competitors.

And, some folks would see vehicles with shape altering appendages driving on the streets of the Elephant's Graveyard. They were just another proposed model with a new look Ford was trying to hide.

Aside from the free vehicles, we got to test some unusual ones. Years ago, we tested total electric Ford Rangers. We had these pickups for several years. Everyone loved them. They would out-drag any police car and were quiet as a muffled mouse. It makes you wonder what the big deal is on getting them on the market now.

Sometimes, Ford's benevolence caused unforeseen problems. Once, Ford delivered five new vehicles for us to test. They were big and they were beautiful. And comfy? They should have been, they were Lincolns. Problem was, as soon as they hit the street with Sheriff's markings the phone started ringing. No damn wonder are taxes are so high, driving Lincolns for patrol cars.

It took a little explaining on that one.

CONVOLUTED LOGIC Ray Barnett, my detective partner at the time, and I had a problem. A merchant on 5th Ave South was boosting profits with a bookie operation. Generally, since it wasn't a crime of violence, we put moral crimes low on the priority list. But, this guy was operating so blatantly, he was probably going to take out an ad in the Yellow Pages next. So, since he was uncool about it, we decided to ice him down. And that presented a problem.

The hurdle was that much of these operations are by phone and we had no bugging equipment. Stuff like that was out of our budget range. So we improvised, and rigged a common portable voice-activated tape recorder to tap the store's telephone lines, hiding the recorder in the store's overhead, drop ceiling. (Don't ask how we got in the store to do it)

Since there was no way to monitor the recorder, we'd go back each night and see what'd been captured on the tapes. One evening we listened to an interesting conversation between the owner and his wife. It went like this:

Wife: "I'm worried about the gambling thing, taking bets. We could get caught, put in jail."

Bookie: "I tol' you not to worry, the cops ain't gonna bother us."

Wife: "Why not? It's against the law."

Bookie: "True, but the cops know you can't stop people from gambling, and whoring, and takin' dope. So it's low priority. Besides, if we don't do it the Mafia will. Don't you think they'd rather have decent folks like us be the bookies, than some crooked Mafia thugs?"

Ray and I laughed, then looked at each other, realizing he was absolutely right.

JUDGE JUDY Don't know how long Judge Judy has lived in Naples but she does. Some of the cops have met her and say she's a sweetheart, not like the tough judge with the rapier wit on TV. I never watched Judge Judy until retirement, and she was one of about fifty that permeate daytime TV--the court shows and those personal injury attorneys trying to get folks to sue everyone. No damn wonder health and insurance care is so expensive.

Howsumever, if you watch Her Honor a few times you'll see why she's number one. Judge Judy is the antithesis of political correctness. She says the things we would all like to say and to the folks who need to hear it. She calls it the way she sees it. As an example.

To a man who'd been collecting disability for ten years for a bad back and yet had a furniture moving business. You are a thief, a scammer. You should be in jail. And to his wife when she tried to intercede, You're a thief too, you knew about it.

Then to a stay at home dad who'd been on public assistance for as long as he could remember. You're a lazy bum who produces children we have to pay for. You should get another hobby.

And to a young couple who moved out of their apartment after trashing it and leaving it filthy with rotting bags of garbage. You're not even human. An animal wouldn't live like that. And it's not that you don't have the time to clean up. Neither of you work, and we're paying for you to be slobs.

One of the great things about being a cop was you could tell it like it was, too. Or, at one time you could.

THE HIGH COST OF VOTE BUYING   Watching all the election shenanigans makes you wonder why someone would spend $120 million, of their own money, for a job that pays a couple-hundred thousand. And who is contributing all that money for candidates and causes.

Working on the Sheriff's Department up in Bashful Beaver, Tennessee I got the answers real quick. Ol' Beaver was a dry county, no hard liquor. You couldn't go into a friendly bar and get a quick snort. And just about every election there was an amendment to do away with that stupidity. And it always failed. Why? Cause there were huge dollars spent to insure that it did.

Most of this money was put up by the churches. Understandable. One could see why hard shells would be against imbibing the evil brew. But the churches didn't really put up the money. The money was given to them by the bootleggers.

Since we dumped prohibition, you can hardy find a bootlegger anywhere. Except communities that never got the word that prohibition didn't work and is over. But in up-tight communities, the bootleggers can thrive and have a vested interest in keeping a county dry. They know folks are gonna drink anyway and they can supply all they need. If suddenly you could buy booze anywhere, who'd need them. So they shoveled out money to the churches for them to do their good deeds for them. And it worked. Maybe still does, I don't know.

Kinda makes you wonder who put up all that money in California to insure the defeat of the marijuana legalization law. Let's see, who would have the vested interest. . .

MEALS ON WHEELS At one time, this vehicle was a common site on the streets of Naples. Pictured here in the Swamp Buggy Parade of 1976, passengers include Aubrey Rogers, Sheriff, and some Explorers, who were one of the primary benefactors of the kitchen on wheels.

The Junior Deputy program, started by Sheriff Doug Hendry, and brought to fruition under Aubrey, also benefited. Aubrey made it a civilian adjunct to the SO, and appointed Earl Hodges as prime-mover. Earl's still there, along with John R Wood, another early board member.

Many Junior Deputies had their first contact with law enforcement as members, camping out with and learning primary outdoor skills from the cops and advisors. And it was a positive experience. Many of the happy campers went on to become cops themselves.

JUST DYING TO GIVE YOUR MONEY AWAY? Watching the political commercials on TV makes you wonder just how stupid they think we are. Of course, with our electing record the answer is easy. That's why in a commercial they'll say anything knowing there is some fool out there that'll believe it.

A friend of mine, Jim Burnett, just sent me an e-mail that reminded me of one outlandish bender of the truth that made a living on his scams for a number of years. We'll call him Slicker Than Willie.

The email showed a small block of wood with this written on it. "Exercise block. Walk around the block twice and when folks ask you if you exercise tell them you've walked around the block twice."

This a variation on Slicker's "Foolproof Fly Killer." Slicker sold these my mail. The ad read "Guaranteed to kill flies. One dollar plus postage and shipping." What you received was two small blocks of wood, one marked "A", the other "B." Instructions: "When fly lands on block "A" strike sharply with block "B." He sold these until the news papers shut him down.

Slicker was not discouraged. It eventually happened in every town he moved to. So, before he'd move on he'd used his failsafe second plan. He placed ads that read, "This is absolutely your last chance to send one dollar to PO Box 123." And the money rolled in.

So when the soap company tells you, for the hundredth time, about their "new, improved" product and you wonder what kind of crap the original your mother used was--after all these years of improving it--you can see where they came from.

Some folks will buy anything. Just look at some of the scumbags we've elected of late.

Editor's Note: As so often happens, readers come up with incidents that compliment my yarns. This one is from Dave Dampier.

Reminded me of the one my stepdad fell for. The ad in the newspaper said "Guaranteed Roach Killer. 100% guaranteed if used as directed."

He received a small package in which were printed directions and a small, sharp, pointed wood stick. The directions read:"Place point of stick on head of roach and press firmly,"

Choir Practice
Session Twelve

GRANDMA We all called June Folsum "Grandma." I was responsible for that moniker. June loved it.

Had the pleasure of working with her at two agencies. First, the NPD where she was June Holtzhausen, married to Don who owned a music store. June was a dispatcher, secretary, matron, and, in reality, the real honcho of the outfit.

She was smart, remembered everything, and had a punch like Marciano. Once, I said something that displeased her and she gave me a sample. I listened to tweety birds for several hours.

June was a daughter in the House family, old-timers in Collier County. Dan House Prairie, in the Big Cypress is named after her father. Her family once ran the old Gulf Hotel on 5th Ave South.

When I was a young Detective, June was the secret of my success. If something happened she'd say, "Ol' so-and-so is probably good for that one." When I asked where Ol' so-and-so could be found she'd give me a look like I'd never heard of The Three Little Pigs, then the address, and say,"Everyone knows where he lives. He's lived there for 30 years.

And poor, ignorant me would explain that I'd only lived here two.

June went on, like so many, to the CCSO where she became the Records Supervisor. Again, June claimed all the ground she stood on and was a superior Deputy.

Grandma left us all too soon. To the regret of many.

Photo courtesy of Chester Keene

TIRE WEASELS An agitated citizen stormed into the CCSO lobby wanting to show something to a Deputy. The duty officer, Capt Crunch, said he'd take a look, seeing it was the only thing except mace that would calm the citizen down.

Outside, the man, D.S. Gruntled pointed to his car parked at the curb. "The tires," he said, "just look at those tires."

Crunch did. "What am I looking for? They look new, right out of the factory."

"They are," D.S. said, "that's the point. I just bought them two days ago at Camelot Tires and I've been ripped off."

Crunch studied the tires again. "I'm gonna need a little help here or I'm goin' back inside."

"Look at the tires on this side," D.S. said, "then on the other. You'll see. It took me a couple days to figure it out. Knew something was wrong but couldn't pin it down."

Crunch took a walk around the car--twice--before he saw it. Then he tried to suppress a laugh, and failing miserably, covered it with a cough.

"It ain't funny," D.S. Gruntled said. "I got a car that's got whitewalls on one side and black walls on the other."

Crunch choked back another spasm. "Did you take them back?"

"Sure. And the salesman said to fill my order--bein' short on tires-- they'd had to use two whites and two blacks. What's worse, he says "What's the big deal? You can only see one side of a car at a time."

Crunch could stand no more, retreating back to his office, D.S. Gruntled in hot pursuit.

After regaining his composure, Crunch made things right with a phone call to Camelot. At first, the salesman was reluctant. But Crunch reasoned with him, explaining that if he didn't straighten this crap out, his weasel ass was going to be looking at only one side of the scenery at a time. The side you could see out of a jailhouse window.

GRUMBLIN' ROADS In the 60's there was a southbound strip of Highway 17, near Zolfo Springs, that talked to drivers. Sort of. Ken Mulling showed me the rumble strip type surface one day when we had case work over around Arcadia.

The idea, Ken explained, was that if you drove too fast over the strips they would vibrate up through your car the admonition: Slow Down. We tried it several times and were only able to coax out an unintelligible grumbling sound. It was a sound, however, that like the rumble strips that jolt inattentive drivers on highways, would get your attention.

After I asked several other old cops if they remembered the thing, and got negative answers, I looked it up on the wellspring of all knowledge, the Internet. Wikipedia says the strip wasn't unique. There have been Musical Roads in Denmark, Japan, South Korea, and the USA. They would hum, when driven over at highway speed, everything from Mary Had A Little Lamb to The William Tell Overture. So, maybe I'm not fantasizing.

Studying on it longer, I seem to remember that after we'd driven back and forth across it a dozen times or so something did finally rumble through my unreceptive skull. It sounded a great deal like: Get a life, stupid.

THE TONY LEMA BOYS

End of the day for the security detail of the 1977 *Tony Lema Golf Tournament* on Marco Island. It's always what the photos don't show that tells the story--like the empty Michelob bottles on the ground from a case donated after they went off duty.

Of course the Deputies had good reason to be in such high spirits. They'd had a good time that day. Hanging out with members of the championship 1972 *Miami Dolphins* and listening to Jackie Gleason crack jokes was pretty darn good duty.

All the cops loved the Tony Lema. As did the athletes.

191

Thanks to Tom Smith and Dave Johnson

From left to right: Bill Padgett, Lloyd Sisk, Steve Hornsby, Acey Edgemon, Dave Johnson and Byron Tomlinson.

THOSE SNEAKY CHAIRS Dave Johnson strikes with yet another diabolical chair chiller. As Dave tells it:

We had a secretary with a ponderous posterior (big butt). She was a sweetheart, but cops can become predatory when there is an opportunity for humor.

We noticed she didn't have a lot of side clearance with the arms of her office chair. It was the old sturdy steel frame kind that lasted for generations. We decided we would psych her into going on a diet by making her think she was gaining weight.

I brought in some large screw clamps and we began squeezing in the arms, a little each night. This went on until she damn near got stuck in the chair --and almost fainted from dieting.

Then we reversed the process! Using a spreader bar, we pushed the arms back out a little at a time until she was comfy again. She thought her diet had worked and all returned to normal.

She later found out what we did but, being the sweetheart she was, never held the station house humor against us.

THE SCENT OF SANTA Chester Keene reminded me of a tale of Christmas Cheer--Cop style. The officers at the NPD decided it would be a nice gesture for one of them to be Santa Clause for the PAL kids. But who could portray the jolly ol' elf?

There were a couple of requisites. First, one of our most likable officers had to be selected, since they'd be working with children, many of whom are afraid of the fat man with a beard. (Some of our cops were gruff and broadcast menacing presence that would terrify Lucifer) And, most importantly, the cop had to fit in the Santa suit.

The obvious choice was a cop we'll call Rumple. Rumple had a grand sense of humor, liked children, and the Santa suit fit him perfectly. Rumple's only possible drawback was that he was a tippler and liked his tan and foamy. But, he wasn't a drunk, and who would know?

At the gala event, the line of children was long and eager, each with a Christmas list. All went well until one wary child climbed on Santa's knee, looked Rumple up and down, took a whiff, and bellowed, "You smell like beer!"

We suppose Kris Kringle slid down that child's chimney early Christmas morn. But Rumple sure as hell didn't.

A SLIPPIN' AND A SLIDIN' Dave Dampier recalled when we wore synthetic fabric uniform pants, that had no traction in the rear quarters, and all the patrol car seats were vinyl. You had to make sure your seat belt was buckled or braking put you into the windshield.

To make matters worse, some joker sprayed the vinyl seat of one officer's cruiser with silicone. When he slid in, he, literally, slid to the passenger's seat.

Chester Keene remembers when the rear seat in the cruisers were replaced with fiberglass models, to hold down the wear and tear by unruly arrestees. For those, taken into custody, who demonstrated they were true A-holes, a dose of silicone was applied to the seat, making the prisoner a ping-pong ball at every stop, start, and corner.

This calls to mind the old platitude: When you get in a peeing contest make sure it ain't with a skunk.

OLD ROCKIN' CHAIR'S GOT ME When she was a rookie at the NPD, my Favorite Dispatcher--later my wife, Sandy--was the victim of dark cop humor. That was a good thing since cops don't tease folks unless they like them. Sandy was a victim of "the chair."

Dispatchers ride a chair almost their entire shift and we tried to buy the most comfortable one our meager budget would allow. But, hoisting butts 24/7 caused them to wear out faster than a fat guy's enthusiasm for marathon running. Until we could get a new one, we made do with regular office chairs.

When Sandy came to work one day, one was waiting for her: a straight-back oak office chair. Since, all the offices were locked for the night, she had to use what had been provided. And she tried.

The cop she was working with, Earl Perkins, was recuperating from a broken leg and had been assigned dispatch duties. He had a slightly better chair, but needed it because of his fracture.

Sandy tried hers, and it was terrible. The seat was hard as a hooker's heart and you seemed to have to brace yourself to keep from sliding out. She brought in a cushion from home and tried that, but it kept sliding out. But being a tough little woman, she kept at at. For almost a week before Perkins confessed.

Sandy had been provided the chair from the interrogation room. This chair had been modified to put the interrogatee under pressure. The front legs had been sawed off a half-inch and the oak seat waxed. You couldn't see the alterations by looking, only by sitting. And then you didn't realize what was being done to you.

After she worked there a while, Sandy found out cop humor is usually a pain in the ass for someone.

WHEN YOU KNOW YOU'RE IN TROUBLE When selected to attended Dick Arther's polygraph (lie detector) school in New York I felt fortunate. Mr Arther was the best in the business. How good? The government had him on an airplane to Dallas to polygraph a fella named Lee Harvey Oswald when Jack Ruby cancelled out the appointment. At the time, he trained most of the CIA and FBI examiners. So you did exactly what Dick taught you to do if you wanted to be successful in the truth verification business.

I found out right away what was important. About one week of the school was devoted to how to use the instrument (polygraph) and five weeks to interrogation techniques. The polygraph was just a doorway to the truth. The truth was obtained with interrogation.

We learned how to meticulously set the stage to induce confessions. To put so much pressure on a suspect that they fell apart like a Chinese automobile. And most of the time it worked. But, there were times when all your devious work failed, and some cool customer was rubbing it in.

Such a slick dude we'll call Cue Kumber. Ol' Cue was a suspect in an aggravated assault--a little rowdiness at a local Knife and Gun Club. Everything was going just to plan. I had Cue trapped in the small interrogation room, his chair wedged in a corner, physically, where he couldn't get out except thru me. He was beginning to sweat. The questions were coming fast and pointed.

One such was, "Have you ever been in the joint, Cue?"

"Yep," he said, "but I was innocent."

"What was it alleged that you did?"

"They said attempted murder. . .that I stabbed a guy."

"How'd they get that idea?"

"Well," Cue began, "I was standin' on the corner, mindin' my own business, cleanin' my fingernails with my pocket knife, when this clown comes runnin' 'round the corner and runs right into my knife."

"Uh-huh," I said.

"Ran into it fifteen times," Cue said, giving me a sly smile. "Fifteen times, right in the back."

Cue then gave a bigger smile and said, "Say, you don't have any coffee do ya? I'm as dry as a camel's cod sack."

I hoped the coffee pot was full cause it was gonna be a long night.

IN THE COMPANY OF BUD TINNEY Bud Tinney was a part-time sports reporter for the Collier County News. (Naples Daily

News, now) And a part-time sports reporter for WNOG. Fact was, Bud would tell you, he was part-time at most everything.

Born under fortunate circumstances, his family owned the island they lived on in New England. Bud still lived there, occasionally, when it got warm up north. He said he spent his youth on the amateur tennis circuit, until his dad decided a reluctant Bud should really go to work and bought him a seat on the New York Stock Exchange. He tried stock brokering a few months--until he found out how valuable the "seat" was--and promptly sold it. Since then he'd been part-timing it.

When I first met him he had to be in his sixties. Small and wiry with a nose like Elmo, and dressed in outlandish golf garb, he was hard to miss. And harder yet not to like. Bud would've fit nicely in any Damon Runyon story.

Bud, and other reporters, liked to hang out at the NPD and we enjoyed having them. There was a desk set aside for when they actually took notes from the reports for a story, but mostly they drank coffee, smoked cigarettes, and BS'ed with the officers.

Bud came in one day with a photograph of him and Richard Nixon. It was taken on a local golf course during one of Tricky Dick's visits and was one of probably a hundred Nixon had taken with anyone who wasn't ashamed to be photographed with him. Bud wanted to borrow an envelope so he could mail it off to Nixon and have him sign it. When he received an askance look, he said, "Dick's an old friend of mine." Uh-huh.

"I'll call him in advance and tell him it's coming," he explained.

"That's the White House," I said.

"I have another number," he said.

Bud was alway telling how many celebrities he knew. Said he'd met them when he was a hot-shot tennis player. We chalked the Nixon thing up to that kind of polluted air.

Until, a couple weeks later, when Bud returned with the photo and an inscription from Tricky Dick about how much he'd enjoyed talking to Bud on the phone, and how much he missed him.

Later, Bud brought in an album with photos of him with the "A" list of Hollywood. After the Nixon thing, it looked good to me.

SANTA'S ELVES IN BLUE One Christmas long ago, two desperadoes were caught in the act of larceny. The culprits: two elderly ladies. Their prize: a Christmas tree.

It was 11 PM on Christmas eve when the two were collared, at a tree lot, surreptitiously stuffing a prime pine into the trunk of their station wagon. The two, short on funds, but brimming with Christmas spirit, were going to deliver it to a nursing home. Explaining the theft, they said they figured, due to the late hour, the remaining trees were going to waste anyway.

Chester Keene was one of the cops who caught them. He, too, was overwhelmed with their misdirected good intentions. After talking to the lot's owner, he struck a deal on a reduced price, the other working cops chipped in, and the ladies were given the tree as a present and sent on their way.

Chester said, looking back, it was one of his best Christmases ever.

Who said Santa's elves all wear red and green?

DOOBIE CANES Lila Zuck, local historian and author of "Naples Oldest Tradition, Swamp Buggy Days" reminds us of a stunt pulled in 1977 to promote marijuana legalization.

Lt. Paul Sireci was opening his morning mail, just before Christmas, when he discovered in a bulging envelope, an extra large, candy cane shaped marijuana cigarette. He wasn't alone.

A group calling itself the "Naples Buffalo Association" mailed the festive doobies to several well known area residents, including the Mayor. They said their purpose was "to show our total disregard and utter disrespect to the antiquated and unjust marijuana laws, we have taken our time--and reefer--to share with these select people in this holiday season, a chance to experience before they condemn."

Getting sent marijuana cigarettes during the holiday season was nothing new, but these candy cane doobies were a unique twist. Problem was cops don't write the laws we just enforce them, some of which we don't agree with.

Paul Sireci laughed, and sent his to the evidence locker. I kept mine for New Years Eve.

Nah, you know better than that.

Thanks to the Daytona Beach Morning Journal.

BUDDY'S GIFT Nothing to do with the cops. Just a story I like to remember now and again, especially at Christmas time.

Buddy dreaded this time every year. Christmas time. Time for you to give a gift to the student in your class whose name you drew. It wasn't that he was cheap or didn't like Christmas. It was that Buddy was poor. So poor he wore clothes that, though impeccably clean, were patches upon patches. Wore shoes with the sole taped so it wouldn't flap.

Most of us were hard up back then, the end of the depression, the war and all, but Buddy made us look like Hiltons.

Buddy drew my name that year, in the third-grade class in Spring Hill, W.Va., and when gift time came he proudly placed a cigar box on my desk. It was not wrapped, festive paper being a luxury he could not afford.

I opened the box and was stunned. It was Buddy's collection of marbles. A collection he loved. The most beautiful aggies he'd won in the marble rings scratched in the playground dirt. And he'd given them to me.

Even at that young age I knew I'd received a special gift. While the rest of us gave something, Buddy had given all.

And, knowing their worth, they were a cherished possession. For about two weeks. The time it took for him to win them all back from me.

Choir Practice
Session Thirteen

ASK WARILY TV commercials are dominated by folks wanting you to sue someone. Or file bogus claims. Or call someone to help you sue someone or file one. No wonder insurance is cost prohibitive and Social Security is going broke.

Now, I have no experience with any of the "Ask" someone deals. Far as I know they could be run by benevolent souls just wanting to help humanity. No ulterior motives. Not wanting a piece of the action. But, I do have experience with one that is no longer around. This is how it worked.

Wally Weasel got in an automobile accident caused by dozing off. He was driving a sports car and weaving down the road. An oncoming driver tooted his horn at the wobbling Wally, causing him--because he was awakened from a sound sleep--to lose control of his Triumph TR3. He drove across a lawn and crashed into the house that belonged where Wally didn't.

In a few days, an ambulance chasing firm gave Wally a call. He told Wally he could help him make a few bucks. Wally explained that the accident was his fault, and he was not injured. The only person who suffered was the home owner, who was knocked out of bed when Wally crashed into his bedroom.

Mr Slim, from the "helper" firm told Wally that fault was just a word, a matter of perception that could be "adjusted." He was so persistent he signed Wally up for the program.

The program involved Wally going to Slim's picked doctor who told Wally where he hurt, when to say "Ow" when he was poked in the right spot. He also gave Wally a series of pain shots that were really just vitamin shots and a nice donut to wear when he went outside.

Then, a lawyer, explained to Wally that he'd been so shaken from the accident that he didn't remember what actually happened. The lawyer told him what did, an absolute lie, involving being forced off the road.

After a few months, Slim's doctor and lawyer received a nice check from an insurance company, Wally's wallet fattened, too, and Mr Slim's company took a percentage.

So, I'm not saying today's "Ask" companies operate in the same fashion, but I'd be particular who I called. Or, you might become a slimy weasel yourself.

WHATEVER WORKS While attending Detective's school at the University of Georgia, I met a personable cop from Atlanta named Jake. Jake was of the Jewish persuasion. Kinda. He said his family were all serious about the faith but he was a slacker. Said he wasn't even welcome at synagog.

Over some excellent Jack Daniels black one night, we were discussing religion, usually a bad practice--especially when drinking liquid stupid. I'd noticed that he had a pendant hanging around his neck that depicted a Star of David. I asked him why, if he wasn't that serious about his religion.

"Not taking any chances I might be wrong," Jake said. Then he flipped over the medal and on the other side was a Christian Cross. He smiled again. "Like I said, I'm not taking any chances."

I laughed.

"And," he continued with a smile, "it seems to work. So far I haven't been bitten by even one vampire."

I recalled that he favored bacon with his breakfast. "No problem," he said. "A priest can pass his hand over tap water and make it holy water. I pass mine over bacon and it becomes a nice Gefilte fish."

I learned early on to be forgiving of religions folks who'd "backslid", as they say back home. One of my favorite uncles was a self-ordained minister. Trouble was, every few years he'd gather up a pretty member of the choir, grab the building fund, and abscond to Mexico. He'd stay there until the fund was exhausted, then come home.

Incredibly, the church always took him back. He had a stock redemption speech he made to them that worked every time. "The Devil is alway working," he'd say. "And if he can corrupt a man of

God like myself, what chance do you have without me?"

Whatever works.

LIES, LIES, LIES The storm over the validity of polygraphs has raged for years. Reviewing the history of the instrument, you can see why. There is a lotta deception in the deception business.

As one story goes, interrogators in WWII made alterations to their polygraphs to squeeze the truth out of Japanese prisoners of war. They altered the ink well, that fed the chart pens, so that the examiner could, on the sly, switch from black ink to red ink during the exam.

During the preliminaries, the examiner would caution that as long as the subject told the truth, the track would be written in black ink. If, however, the subject lied the tracing would be written in blood-- sucked from the attachment on their arm. (The cardio cuff like the one used to check blood pressure)

Then, when the examiner suspected the prisoner was lying, he'd switch to the hidden red ink reservoir and the "blood" tracing would appear. The customer was warned that if he continued to prevaricate the polygraph would suck him dry.

No one's stupid enough to fall for that gag you say? It worked with such effectiveness that it was used throughout the war.

Chester Keene reminds us that you didn't have to go to the Orient to encounter "lie-detector" shenanigans. There were some--in candor I must plead guilty to this--that would seat a prisoner in the front seat of the patrol car and tell them a field lie-detector test was going to be conducted. Then, the cop would wrap the mike cord from the police radio around the subject's arm.

The testee was told that if he lied, the red light on the lie-detector would come on. This light was the transmit indicator, that came on anytime the radio was in talk mode. In this case, the cop would hide the mike in his palm and key the transmit button when he suspected his subject was lying. And more times than not, it worked. And on folks that should know better.

A BAD SPELL This is from Dave Dampier who remembers the days before Spell Check on computers and some of our cops who couldn't spell sugar if they had a mouthful.

One of my early supervisory duties at NPD was to review and approve the written reports produced in the preceding 24 hours. These were typed, with a carbon copy, or later NCR. Both were a pain to correct yet we demanded the best written report possible because they were public records and could be used in court and were seen by the "newsies", who loved to tease us about some of our hobbled Hemingways.

I will say that the majority of our officers were good at meeting the report's factual and information requirements. But, some had spelling ability deficiencies that required sleeping with a Funk & Wagnall's.

Minor misspellings were usually easily corrected and in most cases I just wrote over a misspelled word or two. But, occasionally I ran into a composition that just would not pass muster.

We had a primo investigator who went on to a successful career at the Collier County Sheriff's Office. One of the best! A virtuoso at detective work. He had, however, a tin ear when it came to spelling--just had no feel of how a word should be spelled. If we would misspell a word kitchen, he might try cittshund. In all other respects his reports were perfect.

There was another officer I recall who always "Pulled the car to the crub". He may have been dyslexic, but we didn't know what that was in those days. Another favorite, "Arrived on the seen and fownd".

These were minor things compared to "Officer Fonicks" who we hired as a trained, seasoned, and experienced officer from up north. Officer Fonicks was repeatedly given the task to re-write reports due to numerous misspellings, inadequate sentence structure, and just plain inability to convey facts in written form. One time I sent a report back to him for re-write and that afternoon he was seen in the squad room with his wife at his side, struggling with the task. He later brought the re-written report to my office and I had difficulty reading same. When I tried to point out some of his errors and omissions he said "But Lieutenant I just can't do it".

My immediate and, admittedly, off-hand response was "Well Bob, I would advise you to seek another line of work". The next I heard of Officer Fonicks was when I tried to read his resignation letter.

He was with us but a short time--just a few months. Guess he decided they weren't so picky at the Cincinnati PD so he went back home.

Editor's note: My stuff is spell checked by the computer, my wife, Sandy, and readers. And still things get spelt wrong.

A CLOG IN THE COGS Another example of not being particular about what you say, involved a guy we'll call Rick Janovich, one of the best cops at the NPD. Always there when you needed him, knowledgeable, tough when he had to be, and gentle when he should be. I hated to lose him. Especially, when I found out the reason.

I was working late one night and heard a scuffle in the hallway entrance by the jail. Investigating, I saw Rick picking up a "customer" from the floor. When Rick saw me, he started dusting off the prisoner like he was a new hat that had blown in the dirt. "He tripped," Rick said.

Listening to the A-hole's rant, I could see how a loudmouth like that might "trip" on the way to jail. I went back to work.

After he'd booked his prisoner, Rick dropped by the office. Worried, I guess, about what I'd seen he asked, "How am I doing?"

I gave him an honest answer: "Rick," I said, "you are one of the main cogs in my big machine." Rick frowned, turned and left my office. A week later he resigned and joined the CCSO.

Years later, when we were both working for the CCSO, I asked him why he'd resigned from the NPD. Incidentally, it hadn't hurt him, since he was a Lieutenant with the Sheriff.

"You as much as told me I had no future there," Rick said, "so I left."

"No future?" I said, "you were one of our best officers."

"Then why did you tell me I was clogging up your machine?"

"Rick," I said, not quite believing what I'd heard, "that was a compliment. I said you were the main cog in our machine. A key element."

"Oh," Rick said and never mentioned it again.

Causes you to wonder how many relationships are destroyed because one persons doesn't hear what the other really said.

A LITERAL TRANSLATION Generally, it's a good rule to be particular about what you say. An off-hand remark, taken literally, can have devastating effects. Such was the case when my daughter, Lori, was about ten-years-old and was having trouble with a bully in the neighborhood. She told me the A-hole, an older, bigger boy was trying to "grab" her.

I told her I couldn't be there to protect her all the time and she should do the following. First, stay away from him. Second, if he continued, to let me know and I'd straighten him out. Third, if he actually did grab her, to find the biggest thing she could and hit him over the head with it. The next day she used the third method.

Sean and Kenny, her brothers, and Lori came running into the house." He grabbed me," Lori said," and I found something to hit him with."

"What was that?" I asked.

"This," she said, displaying a length of 1" galvanized pipe. "And I hit him on the head and he fell over in the ditch beside the road and started to bleed."

I rushed to the scene, wondering if she'd killed him and running the headlines through my head: "Chief's daughter takes his advice and bludgeons another child."

I breathed a sigh of relief when we arrived in the combat zone and the victim wasn't in sight. We went down the street to his home where we found him on the front porch with his father, his head wrapped in a bloody towel. Expecting the worst I asked how he was.

"He'll live," the gruff father said. "He's a dumb-ass, you know, and best place to hit him, and not do any damage, is in the head. Nothing there."

But, he was smart enough not to mess with my daughter, Lori, again.

SOFT SUMMER BREEZE Good Ol' Dave Johnson penned this jewel.

It was in the late 70's and I'd been working on an international heavy-equipment theft ring working out of Golden Gate. A prosecutor, from the east coast, had come over to help out. On his introductory visit, we had some comedy I'll never forget.

Prosecutor Ken was a big, tall, macho guy. He was obviously a man's kinda man. I invited him to walk over to the "Blind-Man's" coffee shop for a cup--a sightless person operated the coffee shop in the government complex for years.

Looking for something to drink, he spied a bottle of ice tea on a lower shelf and bent over to get it. When he did, it sounded like someone emptied the magazine on a Burp-Gun. He'd ripped his pants. Quickly straightening and red-faced, he asked me how bad it was. On inspection, I damn near fell over--his entire right naked butt cheek was sticking out in broad daylight! Choking back laughter, I told him he was in deep doo-doo. And the worst part was, being a warm day we'd both left our suit jackets in the office! He had nothing to cover up his now exposed caboose on the long walk back to my office.

We decided the best thing to do was for him to hold up what was flappin' and for me to walk close-step behind him. We could get things sewed up back at the office with my secretary Sandy's help. So here we go, on a busy day at the courthouse, him scooting along with his hand on his ass and me shuffling 6" behind, like some Three Stooges "You're-in-the-Army-now" skit. We were quite a sight.

He explained that he never wore underwear because the last pair he had worn had rotted off him in the jungles of Vietnam. He was a good guy and I felt sorry for him. When I could keep a straight face.

Sandy stitched his problem up and we went on to put several players in jail, as well as run a few more out of the country.

I wonder if he ever started wearing underwear again?

INSTANT FIELD SOBRIETY TEST One of the things about being a Cop that always appealed to me was the uncertainty. Other jobs, when you go to work you have a pretty good idea of what the day has in store. Not so in the Cop business. Your duties can involve anything from guarding the President of the United States to being careful not to get in the middle--and killed--in a domestic disturbance call. Or, you might slap yourself in the face and drink a gallon of coffee to keep awake during a long, uneventful, night. And these nights are the worst.

All Cops find ways to deal with the boredom. Dark humor is usually a cornerstone to these survival techniques. If you can get a laugh out of it, how bad can it be?

Since drunks get on my nerves in a hurry, I had to invent ways to inject a little humor into the encounters. One was an instant field sobriety test, that although unconventional, was indicative of the liquid stupid level in the customer. No walking the line, saying the alphabet backwards, or touching the fingertip to the nose. Just repeat this simple phrase:

"I'm not a fig plucker, or a fig plucker's son. But I'll pluck figs 'til the fig plucker's come."

A drunk will become an instant animal molester. And you'll be chuckling 'til your watch ends.

DAYS OF WINE AND HOSES Dave Johnson sends this tale of hard drinkin' Investigators--whether they could hold their liquor or not. Their names have been changed to protect the inebriated. As Dave tells it. . .

Larry and Durk were having an early Happy Hour. Cops love Happy Hour! You have a selection of free munchies and drinks are cheaper--sometimes free.

In walks a very successful local defense lawyer, we'll call Elton Ego, who proceeds to make the mistake of pulling up a chair to holster-sniff. Lawyer Elton ordered a drink and offered to buy Larry and Durk what ever they are having. Our heros, being stalwart, incorruptible public guardians, immediately ordered doubles of the good stuff.

Elton, settled in, apologizing for the sleazy job he had and explaining that you didn't take what he said in court personally, it was just his job. Larry and Durk commiserated until Elton excused his self, saying he had to call home. Elton, you see, was afflicted with the dreaded disease; Pusieus Whipitus. And being deathly afraid of his wife caused him to leave the table every 20 minutes to call her and assure that he was being a good boy.

It took Larry and Durk one of Doug Hendry's "New York

Seconds" to get the hint and start ordering doubles--on Lawyer Elton's tab--every time he went to check-in with the boss. After the second round, the waitress got sugar plums over the prospect of a big tip and started bringing, without cue, ever stronger doses of Who Hit John.

Now Larry, being older (with a more experienced liver), was able to hang with the incredible rate of consumption. Durk, on the other hand, was a notoriously "cheap drunk" and was glassy-eyed by the third round. This circus went on for a couple hours, until Durk got up to use the Head and promptly walked into a pillar. He excused himself (to the pillar) and retired to the Men's lavatory where Larry found him sometime later, demonstrating how he could sleep, while standing up, at the urinal.

All the fun and games ended when Lawyer Elton got orders from headquarters to get his booty home ASAP. When he got the bill, for the alcoholic hose job, he almost swooned.

Larry did the sensible thing and took Durk to a very early breakfast to try to sober him up. This not working, Larry did the decent thing for his beloved junior partner, and took him home. Of course, Larry was decent but no fool. So, not wanting to encounter Mrs. Durk, he dumped his pal on the front lawn and peeled out before his car could be ID'd.

Thus were the days of old, when good whiskey over-ruled good sense, every darn time. Much like today.

MIRACLE CURE A few years ago Sheriff Don Hunter started a juvenile boot camp in Immokalee. The idea was to turn the life around of juveniles at risk of becoming habitual adult offenders. It wasn't an easy program. The juveniles lived on site and their routine, both academic and physical, was rigorous. The instructors, Drill Instructors, were Deputies who had received training from the toughest DI's going: The Marines at Parris Island.

I was visiting one day watching the induction of a group of "Candidates." The juveniles had been rushed, shouted at, and bedeviled, a common tactic in boot camps to disorientate the inductees and show them who was in charge.

A DI was addressing the group, who were quivering, standing at attention. "Any one here with A D D or one of those 'initial' things."

A reluctant recruit held up his hand. The DI approached him and placed his hand over his head. "You are healed! We don't have 'initial syndromes' here. No A D D, D O P E, B S, any of those things. All you who claim you have them are cured. They are not tolerated."

And they were cured, many going on to complete high school and some entering college!

As Jim Hansen, Commander of the camp said: "No meds prescribed to treat those "conditions" were permitted at the boot camp and we never saw any negative affects from that.

We firmly believed that 99.9% of those kids were lacking in self control and were manipulators. That was borne out when they realized the consequences of not following the rules and staying focused turned out to be worse than if they did. All of a sudden, we had a miracle cure! Can you imagine?"

Wonder, if school teachers were allowed to discipline and control jerks in class, would the results be the same?

Hmmmmmmm. Gonna have to ask my friend Dr Jose Lombillo, a psychiatrist, about that one. It's too deep for me.

LET THE GAMES BEGIN Gail Addison reminds us of some of the dark humor cops use to maintain their tenuous grasp on reality. After some of the stuff they deal with.

An exuberant, young Investigator--who came bounding into the office each day, dove into his chair, then yanked open his center drawer to dig out work materials--was setting a bad example. No job was that much fun!

To put him on the righteous path, his thoughtful associates rigged his desk so the next time he eagerly approached the day's duties there'd be a surprise in store. Using clear fishing leader, they tied each object on his desktop to the back of the center drawer. This included phone, clock, pens, paperclips, blotter, In-Out trays, you name it.

The next day, when Bounder yanked open his center drawer, everything on top raced to the back, then off onto the floor, disappearing from sight. This left Bounder with something really important to do that day. Figure out what the hell had just happened.

No one was safe from the fun and games. Wilma Horrom, a grand lady who everyone loved, used to buy fresh eggs from Steve Riley, who had a agrarian itch and raised chickens on the side. Steve would deliver the eggs to her office.

Wilma'd then write her name on the carton and put it in the office fridge. One day, some of the guys decided this was just too tidy an operation and took the eggs to the kitchen and boiled them. After the dozen had cooled, they replaced them in the carton. Wilma took them home and spent some time trying to crack one, to fry for breakfast, before she figured out what happened.

And when she got to work, she let the culprits know just what she thought of the stunt. Her lecture so chastened the pranksters that it was almost a week before they decorated her Calla Lily with condoms.

Just good, clean fun at the CCSO.

BAD HABIT BREAKERS Deputy Bounder had another bad habit; he liked to chew on pens. And not just his. Any pen he borrowed or made its way into his hands. If he glommed your pen, when you got it back it'd look like a teething beaver had been at it. So, the big-hearted Cops who worked with Bounder--wanting to help him curtail this gnawing compulsion--decided to intervene.

One day when Bounder was sitting at his desk, brow furrowed over some problem, munching on his favorite ballpoint pen, one of his associates walked by and, casually, tossed a photo on his desk. Bounder took one look at the photo, spit the pen from his lips, twisted his face into a mask of revulsion and stumbled to the restroom, gagging, in pre-barf mode.

What was in this photo? For this tale to be complete, you must know. Sorry 'bout that for it's sometimes better not to delve too deeply. Such was the case with this photo.

Pictured was a CCSO K-9, head turned and staring in quizzical remorse at his rear end. Now, let's hope--for the sake of decency and to avoid a PETA sit-in--that what was depicted was the result of trick photography, some primitive form of Photoshop. Otherwise, I shudder to think how the object shown was inserted where it was. There, in the photo, protruding from the poor dog's backdoor, was a ballpoint pen. Bounder's favorite ballpoint pen.

Bounder took to gnawing on his knuckles after that.

Just another example of how the Cop's way of curing you of a bad habit can be as effective as the Hell's Angel's Collection Agency.

HOW MUCH IS THAT DOGGY UNDER THE WINDOW?

Here's a story from Dave Johnson about John Hisler. John is a superior former Deputy who now regularly demonstrates his excellence as an investigator in the private sector.

John and I were working the east end of town when we got a burglary in progress call at an apartment complex. When we arrived, we eased up to the apartment, which was on the 2nd floor. We could see a broken-out window by the front door. All was quiet and it appeared that whoever broke the window was long gone.

John has an innate curiosity which made him an excellent cop. Sometimes of course that nose can get you in trouble. And it did.

The broken window was chest high, and the hole was sizable. Just enough clearance for John's curiosity. He stuck his head inside to have a look around, then said to me "Hey, I smell a dog".

Now there are two kinds of watch dogs. First, the kind that makes so much noise when it hears a noise that the intruder beats a hasty retreat. Then there's the second kind that, when alerted, lays motionless and silent, waiting to rip the ass off the surprised intruder. The dog John smelled was the second type.

No sooner had he mentioned a hairy sentinel, when a bear-sized German Shepard lunged at his mug. The dog had been quietly laying below the broken window, diligently protecting his master's domain.

John is not a small man, and some would've been surprised at how fast he can move when the urge to is upon him. How he got that big head of his out of that window without cutting it off on broken glass is one of those miracles God occasionally uses to demonstrate his love of street cops. I darn near split my trousers laughing.

As for John, he was beset by another urge, too. And left the scene to change his laundry.

COPPOLINO COHORTS Probably the most famous trial held in

Collier County--aside from the Benson case--was for a murder committed in Sarasota. In April of 1967, the Dr. Carl Coppolino's trial began after being granted a change of venue for fear the notoriety could preclude selection of an unbiased jury in Sarasota. Dr Coppolino was being tried for the murder of his wife. He'd already been tried--6 months earlier--for another murder in New Jersey and found not guilty thanks to the brilliant witness cross-examination by his attorney F. Lee Bailey. That charge alleged that Dr Carl had murdered the husband of his lover. The victim had been injected with a chemical that sent him on his way. Coppolino's wife died of the same chemical being injected. What a coincidence!

Ken Mulling and I were assigned chauffeur duty for a key witness, Dr. Milton Helpern. Helpern, from the NY Medical Examiner's Officer, was world renowned. He'd been called in to do autopsies on the exhumed NJ husband, and Coppolino's wife.

In Jersey, F. Lee had pretty much taken the Doctor's testimony apart, one of the key reason's Coppolino was acquitted. Probably for that reason Helpern despised Bailey and badmouthed him at every opportunity.

"A squeaky-chair lawyer," Helpern would say. This from a trick he claimed Bailey employed of finding the squeakiest chair in the courtroom and claiming it for his own. Then, when he wanted to take attention away from the witness, he'd rock in the chair making an annoying racket. (This ploy is originally attributed to Clarence Darrow)

"The worst attorney I've ever seen." he'd say. "Never took a case unless it meant big headlines and an imbecile could get them acquitted." There were those who would disagree, F. Lee being counsel for The Boston Strangler, Sam Shepard, Patty Hearst and, much later, O.J. Simpson.

But, Doctor Helpern got his revenge in Naples. Instead of finding a jury pool of sleepy rustics Bailey had hoped for, he discovered most were retired professional folks, much above the normal for a jury pool. And, there was no way they couldn't have known about the media saturated New Jersey trial and the controversy over the verdict. So, even though Bailey did his best to discredit Helpern again, it didn't take and Coppolino was convicted of 2nd Degree Murder.

F. Lee and Helpern both stayed at the old Golfing Buccaneer Hotel on the corner of Mooringline and US 41. Bailey held court at the bar each evening and was a popular attraction for the locals. Helpern, much the elder, went straight to his room and stayed there. That was probably for the best since it kept the two from encountering each other. I'm sure Bailey would have cooled it, but the old Doc may have gone after him. Seriously!

After the fun and games, Carl is led away to jail in the company of *Sheriff Doug Hendry, Jed Pittman, and Ken Kitchell*

THE COOKIE LADY Police radio parlance can vary, with agencies, from arcane numbers and codes to a simple conversational style. Some like the Tens and Signals, others think they just get in the way and confuse what they were supposed to clarify. The CCSO and NPD have used several different systems over the years.

In the 70's, however, you would hear one phrase on the NPD's radio that was unique to their police comm system: "Good morning Cookie Lady."

This was usually spoken by the officer assigned to a specific zone. And it was common to hear, "Good night Cookie Lady" when the cop assigned to that zone went off duty for the night.

Was this some super-secret code phrase used to baffle radio eavesdroppers? Something concocted to set in motion or cease some covert operation? Nope, it was just a salutation to a nice lady who was a regular listener.

The Cookie Lady was an elderly woman who befriended cops by dropping off plates of the wonderful yummies she baked for the officers who worked in her residential zone. She was a regular contributor and an avid listener. She knew all the officer's badge numbers and shifts and if she didn't hear one of them on the radio when they should be, she'd be on the phone to the PD asking if they were ill or injured. She worried about them and their safety. The officers all knew it and loved her for it.

Yep, everyone loved the Cookie Lady's cookies, but I think they liked her mothering more.

Now, if she had been The Donut Lady. . .

BROTHER BILLY Sometimes, when we elect a President we get an unexpected bonus. That happened with Jimmy Carter. Jimmy was a quiet, laid-back gent who, most of the time, would've slid right through his Oval Office tour with barely a ripple. And would have--if it hadn't been for this brother, Billy. Billy, you see, was a whole different sack of peanuts.

We got to enjoy Billy a lot in Collier County. He made friends and business connections with locals and spent a lotta time in Paradise promoting stuff or just going to parties with his new friends. And, the boy could party.

One of the Sheriff's Office's first encounters with the lovable rascal was greeting him at the Naples Airport. We were to escort him to some local shindig. A respectable number of news media reps were in attendance. Soon as Billy exited the aircraft, he ran straight to plane's tire and peed all over it. Seems the small shuttle plane had no bathroom and Billy was generally full of liquids that made you want to go. In a hurry.

The tarmac wetting gained national attention and Billy, once again, out-newsed his brother.

We were at an auction with him once where he'd been hired to draw a crowd. He'd done a good job, there was a mob to see him. He was holding a can of beer and sipping from it with regularity and real gusto. I noticed the top had been completely opened like you open a can of beans, making it a drinking glass. "Can't get it out fast enough through that regular hole?" I asked.

"Nah," he said, "I opened it up to pour the beer out."

"Pour it out? Thought you loved beer."

"Do. Good beer. But I have this contract with a brewery to pimp this Billy Beer--he showed me the label on the can. Every time I drink in public I'm supposed to drink Billy Beer. But I can't stand the piss so I replace it with whiskey."

Pragmatics, you gotta love 'em.

CW STRIKES AGAIN This bit of history courtesy of former CCSO Deputy Jack Bobo. With additional info from Dave Johnson.

In the early 80's, Charlie (CW) Sanders lost a finger while investigating an incident near the Dade County line on the East Trail. The night before, we were dispatched to the vicinity of the Jet Port because of a "disturbance." Once we arrived, we met with some campers who said that an unknown white male had been causing trouble. He'd left the scene and we didn't locate him.

The next morning, CW--being CW and knowing everybody in his district--

remembered there was a young ne'er-do-well living in that area, on the East Trail, and this sounded like some of his work. CW drove to this scalawag's residence, exited his vehicle, and headed for the front door when two vicious pit bulls charged him. He kicked one, but the other grabbed his left index finger. CW naturally pulled back and the dog bit the finger off, right at the middle knuckle. The dog sat down and spit out the digit.

CW grabbed the finger and put it in his shirt pocket. He wrapped his bleeder in a hankie and drove himself to NCH, about 50 miles away. There, he asked them to put it back on--which today, would be a possibility.

Within 24 hours of losing his finger, CW was back on duty, making his rounds and checking on the welfare of his district. Not once did I ever hear him complain about the amputation. This was CW Sanders, District Lieutenant, Paratrooper, Stuntman, NASCAR Driver, Mentor, and friend to everyone.

CW was the old breed, never worried about overtime, injuries, or needing counseling because he'd seen some blood. His sole commitment was to get the job done. No matter what it took.

PS. About 6 months later, both dogs were found shot, stone cold dead. An unsolved mystery to this day.

GOLDILOCKS AND THE GRATEFUL BEAR Our Goldilocks was a Secretary in the CCSO Headquarters Building at the Courthouse Complex. She was new to the agency, having relocated from the Chicago area. That was obvious from the Bears memorabilia that adorned the office. A typical Chicago Bears fan. Or so it seemed.

When asked about the Bears decorations, she'd tell you that she was really a fan of just one Bear and point out that the souvenirs all bore his autograph.

Why so?

It seems Goldilocks was driving home from work one night and noticed a stranded motorist standing beside his car on the road. Although she knew all about carjacking and that it wasn't prudent to stop, something told her it was okay. So she did.

Pulling up next to the man, she cracked the window and asked if she could be of help. She certainly could, the man said, eagerly. His cell phone had crapped out and he was going to need a tow. Could she make a call for him? She did and the truck arrived in minutes.

Seeing the problem was solved, she said Goodbye and started to drive off. The driver thanked her, then asked a question. "When you pulled over to help me, you didn't recognize me did you?"

Goldilocks was nonplussed. "No, and I still don't know who you are."

The man laughed. "I play professional sports, on TV a lot." Then he told her his name.

Goldilocks recognized the name, and, vaguely, the face but not being a sports fan, couldn't make a connection with a local team. Cubs? Bears? White Sox? Blackhawks?

The man asked for her address, saying he'd like to send her a Thank You card. It seemed harmless enough, so she complied.

A couple of weeks later the Thank Yous started arriving. A signed photo. A jersey. A football. A helmet. And that's how the collection began. She still received something every now and again.

And who was Goldilocks' Grateful Bear? One the most famous. The Bear's big, bad, bone-crushing All-Pro linebacker: Brian Urlacher.

Can you imagine trying to get that guy out of your bed?

POLITICAL PROFUNDITIES Some of the tasteless shenanigans that go on in today's political campaigns reminded Ray Barnett of the local ballot seeking battles from a kinder and gentler time. Well, sorta kinder and gentler.

Doug Hendry was faced with a number of challengers, over the years, who all found out it was a waste of time. In his prime, Doug was so smooth and intelligent and likable you might as well have tried to take Christ's seat next to God. Probably because of that, most of his opponents didn't seem to be very serious--just looking to get their name in the paper.

Back then, a candidate seldom said anything derogatory about the opponent. It just wasn't done, Old Man. They would, however, enlist the aide of their cohorts to spread a nasty rumor.

During one of these "nice guy" speeches a contender against Doug, who we'll call Dozy Dorwin, was so effervescent in his praise of the Sheriff, some had to be wondering why he was bothering to run against such a great guy.

When Doug finally got the mike, he showed the crowd what a swell fella he really was, by thanking Dozy, for the kind words, and reminding him to zip up his undone fly.

A local character and well digger, Whiz Waters, once decided he was just what the people needed in the Sheriff's chair. Whiz's speech demonstrated what "rough" politics were at the time.

He allowed that Doug wasn't tough enough for the job. That what it needed was a hard scale Cracker, like himself. And to prove himself as that person, he challenged Doug to walk across an oyster bar with him--barefoot.

This was no trick for Whiz, who seldom wore shoes and showed the crowd just how tough his tootsies were by striking a match on his bare foot to light his cigarette.

'Course, the voters weren't impressed and smoked Whiz at the polls.

THE DAMOCO TRIANGLE We're all familiar with The Bermuda Triangle, that expanse of water off Florida that has spawned so many mysteries. But, there's another less known triangle that in the early 60's gave birth to a puzzler of its own. It's the dreaded DaMoCo Triangle, named for the convergence of Dade, Monroe, and Collier Counties.

At one point US 41, the Tamiami Trail, bursts right through the triangle on its way to Miami, on one end, or Naples on the other. If your car is long enough, you can be in all three counties at once.

Near that convergence there once stood a roadside cafe/convenience store called The Trail Center. The small building was a popular oasis on the long, barren Trail. You could buy a tasty burger, go to the John, or gas up and stretch your legs. You could also get skunk drunk on the beer purveyed there and many a hunter did before venturing into the woods with their high powered rifles and bleary eyes.

One day two hunters had way too much fun boozing, decided

they didn't like each other, and went outside to settle the score. One hunter, having forgotten what they'd come there to kill, shot the other.

There were several witnesses to the murder, the shooter didn't deny it, and relieved investigators believed the case should be a slam dunk. Until they pin-pointed where shooter and victim actually stood--or lay--in the former's case. Seems the shooter was standing in Collier County, the bullet passed through the air of Monroe County, and struck the victim standing in Dade County.

This conundrum was a head-scratcher. Just where did the crime occur? Was it Collier, where the gun was fired, or Dade where the bullet hit the victim?

Later, old-time Deputy Bill McCrea, who told this tale to Dave Johnson, said the different agencies sweated over that one for a while, finally deciding Dade County should own it. Hell, with all the mayhem going on in Miami they probably wouldn't even notice one more.

THE MUMMY MURDER Occasionally, when folks at the Naples Police Department are going through the old records they come upon oddities--records that look to have been gnawed around the edges. Those are easily explained: rats. But, the pages are also peppered with shot holes like they'd been used as targets in a turkey shoot. What the. . . ? Chester Keene remembers why.

When we were housed in the old PD at 8th and 8th South we used one of the cells as records storage. It was on the women's side and never used for its intended purpose. So, in need of storage space we converted it to a locker.

One day a clerk, Debbie, went back to the cell to retrieve an ancient record. She rapidly returned, screaming that there was a rat in the records.

Dave Dampier went to our armory and got an old .22 rifle and put some rat shot in it. (Rat Shot is a cartridge with small pellets in the bullet end, instead of solid lead, making it a mini shotgun shell)

He took the rifle to the old cell, located the box with the rat in it, and blasted away. Instead of blood and fur exploding from the box, a cloud of dust and shredded paper drifted up. Seems the critter was long dead and petrified, having starved on a City diet that featured too much starch and no cheese.

Everyone got a good laugh out of the Mummy Murder.

And the Peppered Paper Case is solved.

DOUG'S WAY Russ Davis, former CCSO Deputy, shared this story from the 60's, about Sheriff Doug Hendry. Russ did a lot of community relations work for Doug. So much that some thought *he* was the Sheriff. He was so good at his job, Doug once told me "The only guy I wouldn't want to run against is Russ Davis."

Late one evening Doug and Russ were returning from a public meeting and stopped by St. George and The Dragon for a toddy. Having ordered, and relaxing at a table, they were approached by a man Russ said was a typical Miami/New York City criminal type. He could've been in the movies.

The weasel gave his name and said he'd like to have a few private words with the Sheriff. Doug told him to say what he wanted, he had no secrets from Russ.

The intruder was blunt in his presentation. He explained that he controlled "the number's" racket in all the surrounding counties and was interested in invading Collier. It would be very profitable for the Sheriff. Doug looked at the man a long time, silent, then gave a noncommittal grunt and said he'd get back with him.

Russ said he and Doug then left and headed back to the Sheriff's Office. Doug was silent the entire trip. Russ said he was dumbfounded and heartbroken. He'd expected Doug to grab the weasel and put him in the slammer.

When they arrived at the SO, Russ was still stunned. Could he have been so wrong about Doug after all these years? Was he considering taking the bribe?

The Sheriff finally spoke. He waved Russ into his office, handed him a legal pad and a pen. "I want you to write down everything that man said to us in the restaurant. I'll do the same. Make it as complete as possible."

Russ, still concerned, said, "Then what, Sheriff?"

"We're gonna get a warrant and put that son-of-a-bitch under the jail," Doug said.

And they did.

And Russ never worried about his boss again.

DOWN BY THE SWIMMIN' HOLE

Scott Barnett provided this photo of the CCSO Dive Team in the Mid-70's. Pictured, left to right, are *Sheriff Aubrey Rogers, Joe Johnson, Connie Beard, Jackie Kline, Doug Caperton, and Jay*

Green. The group is standing in front of brand new US Diver's gear.

Scott, who became commander of the group, said he was talked into joining 30 years ago by Jackie Kline. He said Kline's romantic portrayal of the team's dives caused him to believe he'd be cruising down to Cozumel to frolic with the parrot fish.

Jackie left out the part about diving in polluted roadside canals, hunting for the bodies of accident victims. And the part about the one-foot visibility--if you were lucky--and that soft thing you bumped into being a bloated cadaver, his hideous vacant eyes locked on yours in the murk.

DIVE TEAM--DEDICATION TO DOOTY Gail Addison reminds us of what had to be the worst--and maybe most dangerous--dive of them all. This was the Sewer Tank Submersion. What?

The SO received a call from the County workers who process sewage and turn it into non-potable water--and other stuff. That's the water used for plant watering. It hasn't been refined enough for human consumption, but it's great for watering medians and golf courses and the like. Homsumever, one of the tanks used in the breakdown and refine process had malfunctioned. Stopped up. They needed someone to dive down in there and find out what the problem was. Either that, or the crap would have to be emptied on the ground, much to the olfactory sorrow of anyone within a three-mile whiffing distance.

This request was not unusual. Civilians wouldn't believe what cops're asked to do. So, Sheriff Aubrey Rogers took it in stride and passed it on to the Dive Team. Who passed it right back. Dive in a gigantic turd bowl? You gotta be kiddin'? But, Aubrey convinced them they should do what they'd been ordered to do. And they did.

The two unfortunates, who we'll call Doo-Doo Dougie and Jumpin' Jack Splash, proceeded to the scene of the slime. There were several tanks involved in the sanitation process. The one, however, that was stopped up was right at the front, where the raw sewage entered.

Making themselves watertight--they hoped--in their diving gear they plunged into the pudding. Fortunately, they quickly found the problem. An errant 2x4 had gotten in the tank and locked the stirring paddle. They removed same.

Exiting the tank, health workers noted that from what was clinging to their costumes, a simple wash-down probably wasn't gonna do it and directed them to NCH for an inspection and preventive maintenance. After a little professional scrubbing and disinfecting they were nearly as clean as non-potable water.

And, I'm sure that when Jack and Doug listen to some politician whining about emergency worker's excessive pay and princely pension plan, they're pretty comfortable that they earned theirs. And it ain't nearly enough.

COUNCIL COMEDY The City Council always attracts a strange variety of ducks. Some mere puppets, hand selected by the rich folks to do their bidding, their autonomy limited to asking for privy breaks and seconding motions to adjourn. Some are pure nitwits. Others you can equate to self-ordained ministers who have heard the "call" and decide they are just what the voters need. Then there're the opportunists intent on lining their wallets by selling out to developers or whomever.

Fortunately, for the community, most are good, decent, folks who legitimately want to accomplish what we really need. And they've done a pretty good job. Just look around Naples.

But, it's the nitwits you remember most. One, who I'll call Erhard Gerbil was the champion numskull. I was summoned to a budget workshop to defend the number of vehicles in the proposed budget. If memory serves, we probably didn't have more than a dozen at the time. Erhard had decided that since we policed such a small area--about sixteen-square-miles-- we could get by just as well on alternative forms of transportation.

Once, Gerbil had asked why we didn't pedal our way to calls on bicycles and I'd explained why. This prompted my book, *I'm Peddlin' As Fast As I Can.*

We were familiar with the budget workshop process. Every year, or at least when the new Council members came aboard, we had to educate them and answer the same questions. Some *incredible!* A couple of examples:

"If your Uniform Officers could stop all the crime, couldn't we fire all the Detectives?" This idiotic question didn't require an answer. Anyone who'd ask it, couldn't comprehend why. And,

"If you only run three shifts--days, evenings, and nights--why do you have to hire more than three officers?"

And it was always difficult to explain to these dopes that some officers didn't want to work 365 days a year, and needed sick time, vacations, training, and stuff.

None, however, could surpass Gerbil for blatant stupidity. He sat with his peers, at the semi-circular Council table, shuffling through a ponderous stack of papers. A slight, sixitish man, he had the scrubbed-pink complexion of a pampered infant. For attire, he favored Naples *haute couture*, the riotous pinks, greens, yellows and plaids of the golfing set.

Poor 'ol Gerbil had caught a dog fish in the gene pool, cursed with the *Who cut the cheese?* grimace of a restroom attendant in a Mexican restaurant. His pained countenance, was in marked incongruity with his vivid and raffish attire. Indeed, stripped of his fine feathers, Gerbil could've resided in a Dickens novel, perched high on a stool at a clerk's desk, green eyeshade shadowing pince-nez glasses, quill pen meticulously inscribing precise numerals in a moldy ledger.

This time it wasn't bicycles. "I've done some more research and maybe bicycles aren't the best way to get this exploding police fleet under control. Are you familiar with the New York City motor scooter program?"

I told him I was. "Yes, Sir. They're using Vespas, I believe, instead of horses to patrol *Central Park.*"

"Horses?" he said. I could see from the dreamy look in Erhard's eyes that I'd made an error. *Horses, huh?* I could envision us hiring wranglers, buying tons of hay, and getting used to saddle sores. So, I quickly added:

"They don't really like or *want* the scooters but had to switch to them because of the Hippies. Seems the Hippies--who were causing all the problems--found out that if you applied a lighted cigar to a horse's, er, private parts, the beast immediately lost interest in police work and became totally committed to becoming a bucking bronco."

A house of laughter caved in on Mr. Gerbil and that was the last we heard of bicycles and Italian motor scooters.

NPD 4TH PLATOON FEB 1972

The NPD 4th Platoon standing tall on the old City Council Building steps. Pictured, from left to right, front row, *Gary Coopersmith, Chester Keene, Terry Massey. Back row, Darwin Muir, Ken Burdette, Frank Baughman, Mike Ashley, John Lester.*

Made in the USA
Charleston, SC
02 October 2012